*Toward a*
CHRISTIAN PHILOSOPHY
OF HIGHER EDUCATION

# Toward a
# CHRISTIAN PHILOSOPHY
# OF HIGHER EDUCATION

*Editor:*

JOHN PAUL von GRUENINGEN

*Philadelphia*
THE WESTMINSTER PRESS

377.8
G 886t
78750

Library of Congress Catalog Card No.: 57–5133

# CONTENTS

## PART FOUR: GOALS

# FOREWORD

C HRISTIANITY has a science of knowledge relevant to the present and valid for the seeker of truth today. Convinced that this is so, Jamestown College, North Dakota, rallied Protestant scholars in June, 1955, for a three-day convocation devoted to outlining a Christian philosophy of education. As it was both philosophical and realistic in conception, the conference dealt both with absolutes and problems of deduction as well as their practical aspects in the world today. The response was gratifying; some 300 delegates from 58 colleges, seminaries, and universities, including some students, pastors, and laymen of different denominations, attended the meetings. In the face of the seeming hopelessness of an age termed post-Christian, the event was a heartening demonstration of vision, courage, and, in the great essentials, of unanimity. Voices were raised that deserve to be heeded.

It is the purpose of this volume to present as a single integrated study the substance of the thinking of the principal speakers at the Jamestown Convocation. Their addresses have here been edited to serve as connected book chapters and have, in certain instances, been somewhat abridged or revised to meet space limitations or to avoid overlapping. The material, however, has nowhere been intentionally changed in its inherent thought or its essential form. It is here arranged under the headings: Theory, Personality, Method, and Goals. These areas were not arbitrarily or indiscriminately chosen. All of them seemed to be crying for exploration, and their nexus is explained by the logical immediacy of each to what has gone before. In other words each in its way involved the next.

As Protestant Christian educators, we are challenged to formulate an epistemology and a world view, relating our education to our common faith. But what are the fundamentals in our philosophy that will regulate the incidentals of our theory? What place shall we assign to the tradition of wisdom in the substance of our education, and what place to man's business with God in the purposes of our education? How shall we resolve the problem of faith and reason? With these and similar questions the studies of Part I are concerned. However, when we consider the functions of mind, the meaning of faith, and the primacy of theory in our present procedure, our thinking will sooner or later be brought to bear upon what is perhaps the greatest and most significant phenomenon in the scheme of things, the phenomenon of personality and its place in God's economy and his eternal purpose. But if Christ is the measure of personality, then what consideration shall this conception be given in the learning process? The question can hardly be answered without an adequate understanding both of the community and of the learner-teacher relationship. Hence the studies of Part II. Then there are the specific claims of the philosophy underlying curriculum, materials, and methods, as well as administration, which deserve special examination. Part III is devoted to an investigation of such claims. Part IV closes the volume with an appraisal of the goals of Christian education and the marks of a Christian college.

Everyone interested in Christian education, every student and teacher, pastor and layman, desirous of revaluating the meaning of Christian philosophy in the light of modern scholarship and the place of such a philosophy in contemporary education should find in this book invaluable help and inspiration. It is hoped that these studies may help to revitalize Christian higher education and confirm those blessings cherished by all Protestant denominations. The boards of Christian education of the different Churches will find here a chart and compass for committing our academic procedure and life to the Christian higher way. As a textbook for college and seminary courses in religious education, this volume offers rich material and challenging observations. Using the principles it outlines, college faculties could be stimulated to form a Christian philosophy of education for their own college. The study provides for all imaginative students of Christian philosophy the kind of supplementary reading that is conducive to purposeful discussion. It should be useful, moreover, for pastors, acquainting them more adequately and fully with the problems and ideals of present-day Christian higher education, placing at their disposal an instrument for the topical study of vital issues with which many church groups can profitably occupy themselves. It is a book for every co-worker in the Kingdom who would witness to a secular world the validity of the Christian commitment in the freedom of learning.

# PART
# I

*Theory*

# I

# THE NEED: A WORLD VIEW

## Edwin H. Rian

M ORE and more attention has, fortunately, been given of late
to the needs, values, and promises of Christian education. It is
axiomatic that we must have a sound philosophy of education. However, the philosophy of any kind of education, including the Christian kind, is one thing; while a certain kind of philosophy, such as a
Christian philosophy of all education, is quite another, and logically
it comes first. We propose to occupy ourselves here with the latter
of the two concepts, without ignoring the former, and may well begin by admitting some problems of terminology that plague us. We
face them when we would order our thoughts abstractly and de-
ductively with respect to first principles, and when we would address ourselves practically to our environment.

Let us admit that the term " Christian philosophy " is probably
more explicit to its adherents and opponents alike than the term
" Christian education " has become. This fact is not without its significance. We may speak of a Christian philosophy of life, of law, of
government, of society, and of many areas and enterprises other than
education, and we know that it is always the philosophy of salvation and reclamation (which is the source and end of hope), that it
is always the philosophy of the Golden Rule (which is the fruitage
of faith), and that it is always the philosophy of the perfect ideal in
love and charity, which is Christ. When the scorner cries out that
Christianity has not yet been tried, he betrays among other things
that he knows well enough what it is really about. On the other
hand, the term " Christian education " is frequently if not prev-

alently equivocal. To its foes it implies nothing more than an attempt at indoctrinating or proselytizing in an academic environment; to the neutral observer it may suggest whatever chapel activities and "foundation" projects are sponsored by the Church at colleges and universities; to the casual user of the term on the campus it may denote primarily the courses in Christian religion listed in the catalogue; to the more discriminate it may mean all good steps, experiences, and provisions in the education of the Christian man. In recent critical literature it has repeatedly been pointed out that education is not automatically and necessarily Christian when Church-related; neither is it *ipso facto* secular in the sense of antispiritual when it is secular in the sense of nonparochial. For our present purposes Christian education signifies education consonant with Christian philosophy as expounded above, whatever the type of institution or level of work where such education is attempted.

At this point a word of further restriction is in order, lest we spread ourselves too far. Although it is our task to search and understand a Christian philosophy capable of informing all education, our immediate perspective is confined to higher education in the Christian college, which even outwardly must differ from the purely secular school. The latter does not take cognizance in all learning of the implications of theology, understood in its true and legitimate sense. It is the opportunity and the function of the Christian college to do so. Because of the very absence of theology from the curriculum in secularistic education, this legitimate discipline has actually come to be regarded as intellectually suspect. Yet today it is again a vitalizing branch of scholarship and more fruitful than it has been for centuries. The serious study of God and his purposes could well be made central in all teaching and learning, even as it must illuminate the common task we have in hand in clarifying our approach toward a Christian epistemology and world view.

We should be hopelessly unrealistic, though, if we regarded our task essentially as one of unfolding abstract deductions without reference to time and place. We are in the world, though minded not to be conformed to it; we must deal with changing situations and menacing forces as well as with constant relationships and eternal absolutes. It is important that we understand certain non-Christian and anti-Christian powers which are striving tremendously for the mastery of man. Without an informed awareness of the threats to the faith that has given us our freedom, we could hardly promulgate a Christian philosophy of education adequate for and suited to the age in which we live. However, with constant benefit of alert intelligence in the very fire of conflict, we should be able to forge on the anvil of our common evangelical experience an educational theory that will meet the test, because it recognizes absolutes in standards, and because it is relevant to our day.

Two world views are struggling for supremacy in modern civilization. One is centered in man and leads to enslavement; the other is centered in God and leads to freedom. Foremost in espousing the anthropocentric view are the proponents of Marxian Communism and the champions of secularism (defined here, with Webster, as an educational philosophy that rejects every form of religious faith). Determined in defending the theocentric conception of the world and of life is Christianity, or the community of believers in Christ. Thus two life systems are diametrically opposed the one to the other, and there can be no compromise between them.

Communism is the more aggressive of the two man-centered systems of thought and has succeeded in assuming a commanding position not only as an economic scheme and as a political order but as a world view embracing all aspects of life. At its base is dialectical materialism, a complete system of doctrine which attempts to explain the meaning and the end of man's existence. It is a plan of salvation in which the mediator of man's redemption is the proletariat. It can be observed that the whole system results in the deification of man and the denial of God.[1] Secularism, on the other hand, without troubling to deny God and proceeding as though he did not exist, employs methods more insidious and produces effects more dangerous for modern culture than those of Communism have been. As a widely accepted and influential philosophy of education it has been boring energetically from within, destroying the vitals of Christian civilization. Secularism as an academic habit or educational pretense leads to naturalism as a tenet, which holds that there is no order beyond nature. The anthropocentric world view of the secularist finds expression in every area of modern life. In education his achievement has been experimentalism with its emphasis upon experience as the norm for society and the individual. To be sure, the contributions of experimentalism in methods of education and in a proper utilization of student abilities and interests must be admitted; so also must be its pernicious influences. In art and literature the secularistic view has resulted in a false realism. In morals it frowns upon any objective standard of right and wrong. It permeates Western culture and controls the daily living of millions.

These two man-centered world views imperil Christianity. A half-way answer in the form of individual Christian doctrines will not suffice. We must reply with intelligence by pitting principle against principle, world view against world view, and system against system. In truth, we must respond with a life and world view that is all-embracing in thought and far-reaching in vision. It is in the face of these challenges that we must formulate a sound Christian philosophy of education for our day and age.

## The Roman Catholic World View

The threat of a man-centered world view and the necessity of coping effectively with its essential error is recognized by Roman Catholics. In the philosophy of Thomas Aquinas they have a workable system of thought which has served them for more than six centuries. The Renaissance and the Reformation dealt Thomism an almost mortal blow, so that for several hundred years it lay prostrate, but today Neo-Thomism and Neo-Scholasticism have revived Roman Catholic education. At a time when attacks upon Christianity are made on every front of thought and life, Neo-Thomists are prepared to reply with a definite and inclusive life system, by which they diagnose and confront the evil of the day. They declare that modern culture is plagued by disunity, lack of direction, and superficiality; that life today is in all its phases atomistic — art living for art's sake, knowledge for knowledge's sake, and business for business success; that science, instead of bringing the perfect life, has produced disillusionment and skepticism; that the depth and the direction of

life are gone, and that in their stead are confusion and the demorali-
zation of human thought. If the present trend continues, this world,
it is feared, will become inhabitable only by beasts or by gods.[2] But
man desires unity, meaning, and a goal for existence; hence, it is
reasoned, civilization must be grounded upon a faith in an ultimate
divine society which transcends all governments.[3] The apologia of
the Neo-Thomists is not merely that we re-examine and restate the
formulas of Aquinas, but rather that we imbue ourselves with the
*philosophia perennis* that they find intrinsic in him. "Use the spirit
and method of the Angelic Doctor," they say, "in the light of the
problems of the day." With this conviction, aided by the findings of
modern science, they have built a Roman Catholic world view en-
compassing education, sociology, physical and biological science,
history, government, economics, journalism, agriculture, the fine
arts, and even jurisprudence.[4]

### THE NEED FOR A PROTESTANT WORLD VIEW

In some points we Protestants are in accord with Thomists. We
agree that God has revealed himself in the works of his hands, the
physical universe. We hold that God is the source of all truth, including the truth we can arrive at by the honest and methodical
study of the works of his creation. We agree that knowledge depends upon the objects to be known, upon the knower, and upon
some means of relation between the two — since man contacts the
outer world through sense stimuli, by which he comes to know its
objects. However, we must reject any system of mysticism or rationalism which would make man intellectually autonomous or his
mind the source of truth. We discern the noetic effects of sin, that is
to say, the stultifying effects of sin upon the intellect, and we maintain that without the renewing power of God man cannot have an
adequate and trustworthy knowledge of what is good and true,
hence, of reality or the universe. "The natural man receiveth not
the things of the Spirit of God" (I Cor. 2:14). "The carnal mind is
enmity against God; for it is not subject to the law of God, neither
indeed can be" (Rom. 8:7). These are verities to which due regard
must be given. We know that we must not place too much confidence

in unaided reason, nor yet too little, when reason is aided by revelation, and we avow that we may not create a false dualism between God and nature, construed as "simple nature" and not revelation of God.

The question must be raised, Is there any need for further limiting a Protestant world view? Is not our evangelical witness proof of our devotion to one body of principles? Are we not all heirs of the Reformation? To be sure, the beginnings of a life-and-world system are inherent in Calvinism and to some extent in Lutheranism, but as far as any well-worked-out *Weltanschauung* is concerned, there is none. This lack is patent in practically every field of endeavor. For example, in education we have as Protestants no express educational philosophy and as a result no worth-while textbooks disclosing the evangelical point of view. In the politico-economic realm, where the battle is so furious at the moment, Roman Catholics enter the fray armed with Pope Leo XIII's encyclical *Rerum novarum,* on the condition of labor, or Pope Pius XI's encyclical *Quadragesimo anno,* on reconstructing the social order, while as Protestants we do not present a united front.

It is true that the genius of Protestantism precludes the imposition once for all of any authoritarian system or view. The right of private judgment and the witness of the Holy Spirit in the heart of the Christian are precious assurances for us. Furthermore, the conception of the priesthood of believers and the affirmation that the Word of God is our only infallible rule of life and conduct are convictions that should remain inviolate at the very heart of our faith. Nevertheless, Protestantism must stand correction where it has gone astray. We may not cloak the sin of our divisiveness, which has as its consequence haphazardness and waste of effort, in our cause. It may be argued that Protestantism has, indeed, valiantly approached the problems of labor and management, of race and caste, of home and family, of childhood and youth, and of many others in its own effective ways; nevertheless, we must admit that it could have been done better with greater unanimity, with better mutual understanding, with more reliance on Biblical wisdom, and with deeper humility. Surely Christianity cannot be circumscribed. We know that

finite man is not capable of comprehending the whole truth and
that as soon as he asserts the finality of his theory, he misses the
truth about reality. The most we can do is to state principles of truth
with approximate reality. But we are persuaded that evangelical
Christianity has wholeness and consistency of thought, that it answers the question of man's place in the world, and that its system
of thought encompasses the universe. Fortunately, more and more
leaders have come to appreciate the fact that as a religion it does
lay claim to every sphere of culture and furnishes man with a
rationale for the whole of life.[5]

Various proposals for a Protestant *Weltanschauung* have been presented. W. C. Bower contends that Protestantism stands at the
crossroads. It must choose either to return to authority or to go
forward with empirical and experimental thought for religion and
life. Protestantism, he reminds us, stems from two sources, the
Renaissance and the Reformation. The Renaissance was a reaction
from unity and authority to freedom and individualism, with a focus
upon the world of nature and of man. It emphasized inductive
reason and experimentation, which became the fountainhead of
liberalism and the watershed of history. On the other hand, the Reformation was a reaction against orthodox Romanism and a revolt
against ecclesiastical practices irreconcilable with the doctrine of
salvation by faith and the primacy of the Bible. Protestants have
tried to live in two worlds, an anomaly which has resulted in their
sectarianism and uncertainties about authority and neglect of the
ethical implication of religion and its relation to secular culture.
Protestantism must come to terms with these tensions and choose
the way it will go. What Bower advocates is the radical view of experimental thought which would preserve the enduring values of
orthodox tradition — such as the deep tragedy of human life, the
significance of human experience beyond the immediate scene, the
unity of experience against atomism, an account of the irrational
elements in experience — and the sense of security freed from the
dated and outmoded formulas of orthodoxy.[6]

Reinhold Niebuhr, in his two-volume work *The Nature and
Destiny of Man,* takes to task liberalism and its optimistic view of

man. After a critical appraisal of what he thinks are the inadequacies of both orthodoxy and modernism, he concludes that a proper understanding of man and of the world can come only from a synthesis of the Renaissance and the Reformation. In the Renaissance life was filled with indeterminate potentialities. Every cultural task, every social problem, and every spiritual relation presented new possibilities of the good and the obligation to realize them. On the other hand, the Reformation showed that justification by faith is necessary, and that it is impossible to complete life or to eliminate the final corruption of humanity. However, the Reformation practically forgot sanctification in its eagerness to emphasize justification by faith. We must bring the Reformation and the Renaissance together in a grand synthesis.[7]

Another solution for a Protestant world view is offered by W. C. Morrison and H. N. Wieman. Morrison agrees with Neo-Thomism's contention that the stream of life has been poisoned by Descartes's emphasis upon man's reason. This opened the way to humanistic empiricism and eventually to naturalism, socialism, class conflicts, economic individualism — in a word, to secularism, and atomistic irresponsibility. However, Protestantism, he avers, is no longer running in the Descartes-Locke-Hume-Kant-Comte-Spencer-Dewey stream. Protestantism is flowing in another direction. It has more in common with Thomism than with Locke. Man is no longer the center or the end of the process. God is in charge and man is a coworker with God in the creative process. The purpose of its philosophy is not to prove the existence of God, but to explain his ways and to define his character. The gap between the ideal and the real, between mind and matter, and between man and nature is closed by regarding man as having intelligence and ideals that are an integral part and an instrument of the real. This is the essence of the new Protestant life-and-world philosophy as it is championed by Morrison and led by Wieman.[8] We acknowledge their attempt to relate Christianity to culture and to the world. However, we believe that the most promising hope for a Protestant life-and-world view lies in a direct approach to the revelation of God in Christ in the Bible and in a concerted return to the Reformers, to Augustine, and to Paul for our lessons in shaping views in given times and places when serving as instruments of the Holy Spirit. But before we go to the altar we must heal our divisiveness. The community of the Godhead is needed to manifest in all its implications the relation of Christianity to the world. The time has come for the proof of our concord in the great essentials. We may not declare our views in esoteric language: we may not designate them to be " Christocentric " as opposed to " theocentric," or vice versa. The underlying principle is the revelation of the triune God as Creator, as Redeemer, Lord, and Judge of history, and as Comforter and Sanctifier, that he may be appreciated and worshiped in his fullness. " For of him, and through him, and to him, are all things: to whom be glory for ever " (Rom. 11:36).

While some Protestant scholars have taken steps toward a world view, others have labored at perfecting a science of knowledge that is true to the genius of the Reformation and to the Scriptures, and serviceable as an instrument in our hands. Richard Kroner, Nels F. S. Ferré, Erich Frank, and Emil Brunner have all concerned themselves with epistemology and the relation between faith and reason, and have all stressed the Reformation principle of the primacy of faith.[9] We think also of men like H. Dooyeweerd and D. H. Th. Vollenhoven, followers of Abraham Kuyper of the Netherlands, who in contemplating the philosophy of a Christian world view have wrestled with its intrinsic problem of epistemology.[10]

In sum: A Christian world view is not only an intellectual concept or a cold metaphysical doctrine but the expression of a conviction. The cardinal principle inherent in the Christian faith is that Christ is God incarnate. The preparation, the fulfillment, and the consummation of Christianity is Christ, in whom the Creator and the creature meet, through whom the transcendent God is sovereign in creation, in redemption, and in history, and in whom the infinity of the Spirit becomes definitive, understandable, real, and personal. Without a science of knowledge we cannot explain the objective truth and the subjective meaning of the revelation of God in Christ. Without system we can neither relate nor reconcile God and nature, faith and reason, hope and reality. We cannot have a sound world view unless we construct an epistemology. Man searches out and describes the mysteries of the universe in signs and formulas his mind can understand; he can contemplate the verities of revelation only in the symbols and terms of its own language; he seeks and finds peace and reassurance by approaching his covenant God in an I-Thou relationship, and he learns of eternal truth in certitude and spiritual serenity only as the Holy Spirit confirms it in his heart.

A world view for Protestants cannot be superimposed, but it can be firmly founded and built on the rock which is our common faith. Here then lies our current problem and our propitious opportunity. May we proceed from our world view to the task of relating it to principles of education.

### RELATING WORLD VIEW TO PRINCIPLES OF EDUCATION

Once we have accepted as valid a Christian thought system and philosophy of life, we are bound to use it as a key to meaning and unity in all education. Once we are committed to a Christian world view, we are charged to let its light shine on any and every theory of education. Once Christian principles of education in accordance with Christian philosophy as defined above are established, they should facilitate the application of Christianity to all aspects of society. We should then confidently look forward to greater stability not only in the Christian college but in all education. We join Cailliet in the earnest desire that theologians, philosophers, and leaders in many other areas of knowledge may co-operate in formulating a Christian culture.

Although there are many theological expressions of Christianity which have resulted in division within Protestantism, yet underneath these differences there lies one faith that undergirds the whole structure of genuine Christianity, the chief cornerstone of which is the Lordship of Jesus Christ. The call is ours to see eye to eye in a common cause, to work shoulder to shoulder at a common task, and to confront one another face to face over a common world view. We have the strength of great unity in the midst of diversity. Our Protestant allegiance is broad enough to enunciate a philosophy of education that should be useful to any Christian groups, though they vary according to denominations and types of schools. The responsibility for keeping fluid the manner of stating and the method of so applying the key proposals that they will have meaning and give unity to the learning experience of our students must rest with a constantly working staff. It must scrupulously avoid pietism on the one hand and a rigid scholasticism on the other. With resolute endeavor to operate faithfully and intelligently with Christian principles applicable to all situations, we should contribute markedly to a better integration and a clearer direction of Christian education.

# 2

## A PROTESTANT THEORY OF EDUCATION

### *Joseph Haroutunian*

IN THIS chapter, Christian education means education according to the Christian faith. It does not mean the teaching of Christian beliefs or doctrine, but teaching conducted in the light of the Christian understanding of human beings, their nature, their powers, their destiny.

Education is a public concern. It affects not only the lives of men as individuals but also the common life of a society. Hence, educational institutions have a grave responsibility toward the country in which they exist. In our democratic country the schools are responsible to educate the young so that they will be informed and enlightened, considerate of their neighbors' rights, and mindful of the common weal. These qualities, as well as others such as integrity, benevolence, and love of liberty with justice, require a proper education.

But a " proper education " is not easily defined. Much of the time it seems hardly to be a problem. When we consider reading, writing, and arithmetic, and even science, history, and art, we realize how much of education is and needs to be teaching and learning in the traditional and common meaning of these words. It is no wonder, therefore, that our educators are so often interested primarily in matters of method and process which shall make the pupil's learning of a given subject most thorough and effective.

However, no educator but a pedant can long evade questions that have to do with the aims of education. It is all very well to teach language, or mathematics, or history. But one must have a sense of

" What for? " Reading is clearly instrumental to communication among human beings, the enjoyment of literature, a good position in society, and other ends. Mathematics is essential for the study of the physical sciences. History is indispensable for understanding the present. Actually science, arts, and history are, when taught in a given way, interesting per se, but educators are not satisfied with these studies as ends in themselves. They hope that the several subjects in the curriculum are " useful for life." Education is expected to exercise the student's powers; to discipline his mind and body; to train him for meeting future exigencies with success, to find a useful occupation, and to be happy both in self-development and in a place of usefulness and honor in the community. In short, education is expected to produce citizens who are cultivated and capable of some social good.

In spite of the several schools of thought on the kind of education that will produce such salutary results, good sense enables the more judicious educators to recognize that theory and practice, discipline and freedom, book learning and experiment, are all contributory to a well-rounded schooling. Everyone should recognize that theory without practice is futile, and practice without theory is blind. Everyone should know that freedom without discipline is wasteful, and discipline without freedom is deadly. A " liberal " education that is impractical is frustrating; practical education that neglects the " liberal arts " makes for stunted growth. Liberal education must be validated experimentally, and experimental education without the benefit of the tradition of human experimentation is wrongheaded. In my judgment, what we need is not more theories of education, but teachers with good sense who are able to make use of the theories that we do have. Good teachers come out of almost any school of education, provided there has been some reflection in the learning process. So, I think, in our pluralistic society, we can afford to have idealists, realists, empiricists, experimentalists, classicists, and others, each group contributing its share to an educational process which is enriched by them all — so long as the several schools of thought are represented by good thinkers and not by narrow-minded people. A good idealist is worth a hundred poor empiricists, and a good classicist is better than a dozen fumbling experimentalists. This I say in spite of the fact that I am prejudiced in favor of experimentalists and against idealists. The important thing is to have a number of intelligent theories of education engaged in fruitful controversy, enriching our total educational process. Let each teacher prefer the one that his active mind favors without being blind to the excellencies of theories that seem to him less adequate. This I think is the intelligent and fruitful way, and the one most in accord with our American ethos.

It is with the above remarks in mind that I propose a Christian theory of education that will bring out the responsibilities of the Protestant Churches in this field and the contribution they might make to education in our land. I hereby disavow the totalitarian, monistic, exclusivistic, imperialistic, and therefore deadly claim that the theory I propose is the only one that is good for education in our country. But I do say that without an adequate Protestant theory of education, there is a lack which may well have dreadful consequences for the individual and for society.

### A Tradition of Wisdom in Education

Let us start with the question that Meno puts to Socrates, at the beginning of Plato's *Meno:*

> "Can you tell me, Socrates, whether virtue is to be taught or whether it is acquired, not through teaching, but through exercise and habit; or whether it comes neither by exercise nor yet by teaching, but is by nature with those who are possessed of it, or comes to them some other way?"

Now, by virtue, Plato meant the ability to do that which is good. But as he defined the good in terms of the triad of the beautiful, the true, and the good, he defined virtue in terms of wisdom, courage, justice, and magnanimity. Virtue was for Plato a human ability or power. The purpose of education was to stimulate a young man to exercise such powers as he possessed. On its intellectual side, education enabled the pupil to recall, to bring out as idea, what was already there in the mind. On its practical side, education led him to acknowledge and practice the several virtues. Since virtue involved science and right views, it had to be taught. But it could not be taught except by way of bringing out what was already in the pupil. The teacher was, in the process of education, simply the midwife. The realization of virtue depended ultimately upon a " divine portion or allotment." The fact is, as Socrates and Plato saw, that virtue is no necessary consequence of education, even under the best of teachers.

We must notice, first, that the aim of education according to Plato is virtue, and the end of virtue is individual and social good. I think with this view our educators in general agree. Health, wealth, strength, beauty (*Meno, 87*) do not constitute the good. The good inheres in the soul, and the aim of education is to realize the good of the soul, which consists in the exercises of the several virtues. Important though health and wealth are, a man's life does not consist in them. They are conditions of the good, but they are not the good. Hence, it cannot be *the* aim of education to teach men the rules of health and the means of acquiring wealth.

In more modern terms, the aim of education is, as generally recognized, the self-development and realization of a human being in his social and physical context. Each human being is endowed with certain capacities for power and enjoyment. These capacities are intellectual, aesthetic, moral, and social. The aim of education is considered to be the richest and many-sided fulfillment of such capacities and the creativity and self-realization and happiness which follow from such fulfillment. Of course, there is much that has happened since Plato wrote the *Meno* and the *Republic*. Our minds and feelings are more expansive and less disciplined than those of the Greeks. Still, it is a fixed point, with them and with us, that the aim of education is a rich life arrived at by a maximum fulfillment of human nature or man's native capacities. We recognize, as did the Greeks, that the powers of the soul as well as the powers of the body have to be developed; and many of us who are enlightened agree that knowledge and virtue are superior to health and wealth. Such at least is the view of those who advocate a classical and liberal education, and those who are experimentalists, or empiricists, agree. The quarrel between the traditionalists and the progressivists in education (apart from some apparently unavoidable slander) is not so much in their several aims as in their views of method, process, emphasis, and the like.

I should like to make clear that I am in profound sympathy with accumulated educational wisdom in our culture. I am as much of a humanist as the next man, and can see the good life as nothing else than the realization of man's natural capacities or powers. I am Greek enough, and I hope rational enough, to insist that the good for man is to become what he is by nature. This is a simple point, but I would like to rub it in for those who are so benighted as to think that it would be good for a flower not to be a flower, for a horse not to be a horse, for a human being not to be a human being. God made all that he made and saw that it was good. He made a man to be a man, as he made a lion to be a lion. It is a contradiction in terms to think that the good of a man is not to be a man. Sometimes the way pious man-haters talk about goodness or salvation, one would think that God had made a terrible mistake when he made us human, and that it were our business to turn people into counterfeit angels. (By the way, I think this piece of perversion has done incalculable damage in so-called Christian schools.) Since God made man man, there can be nothing more right, or good, or excellent, than that man should live as man. It is good to be, and not good not to be. It is good to be what one is, which is to be; and not what one is not, which is not to be. We cannot dispute this simple dictum of good sense without exposing ourselves to self-destruction, which is evil. To be is good; not to be is not good (allow me a bit of prejudice); and that is that. Therefore, education that aims at a human being's self-fulfillment in his social context is a sound proposition.

## Toward a Christian View

The question, of course, is, What is human nature? Here we are looking into a deep, and we need to be as humble about our understanding as we are eager for the truth. But I take it we have a right to begin where we are. I am a Christian theologian, and I have no alternative but to begin with the doctrine that Jesus Christ is the true man, or, in other words, that he is my own and all men's true nature. The essence of man as God made him, man as he must be if he is to be himself, man in his original endowment and ultimate self-realization, the aim and goal of education, the man whose existence means the good society, is Jesus of Nazareth, the Son of David. I am a Christian, and one is not a Christian unless one acknowledge and confess that Jesus Christ is man in his goodness.

Now if Jesus be the true man, then I am untrue. Wisdom, courage, justice, temperance, magnanimity — in short, " virtue " as I find it in Jesus — is my own true virtue, the expression of my own humanity; but strangely enough though also inescapably enough, it is not a simple possibility of my " nature." The virtue that nailed him to the cross is not a simple potentiality of my life. I recognize that virtue, humanity, justice, friendship, as described by Plato, is natural to me. When Socrates teaches me, I " recollect " it, and assent to it. I admire it and am impressed by it. I even think, given enough " moral influence," I might practice it, more or less. But when I confront Jesus Christ, his gospel and the law of love that goes with it, I receive a shock. When I face the teaching of Jesus, the famous Sermon on the Mount, I am not lured as I am when I read a Socratic dialogue. I am at once overwhelmed and actually repelled. I say: " But this is not natural! It is not possible. It is not even desirable, since it will land me on the cross! " " This does not mean life," I say; " it means death." I must die to myself if I am to be myself. If Jesus Christ is my own true humanity, then I can be my own self only by becoming changed into a nature which is my true self but not my, let us say, " empirical " self. It is not a simple matter to be myself, to be my real self, to attain " self-realization." In one sense, I must grow, develop, find fulfillment. With the help and example of my teachers, I must exercise my powers and actualize my potentialities. All these wise men since Plato were not, of course, dreaming dreams and talking nonsense. But then, they did not have to put up with Jesus Christ. Even while some like Plato recognized the mystery of education, they did not see, they were not constrained to see, that beyond and deeper than the growth of a human being, his learning by theory and practice, by the influence of his fellow men, there is the miracle of denying one's " nature " in order that one may find it.

Our theories of education, whether they be traditional or experimental, classical or romantic, have this in common, that they take no serious view of *education as conversion,* or being made over as a personality. I neither minimize nor deny education by formal teaching, personal influence, discussion, and experiment. I know that there are values in traditional and progressive education, and I prefer the latter, especially for younger children. But I cannot ignore the lesson of Scripture and the work of the Holy Spirit which together establish the ultimate experimental truth that if I am to live in the freedom and justice and integrity and humility and love of a human being as I find these in Jesus of Nazareth, I must be changed in the core of my being, changed into a human being, changed in mind, will, affections, in perspective, motive, and purpose, in my hopes and fears, in my joys and troubles, yea, in my very virtues and competences.

We know that the simplest procedures of teaching grammar or arithmetic depend upon the teacher's larger or deeper aims with regard to the child's development. Grammar must be taught with an eye on literature, and arithmetic with an eye on the sciences. The teaching of art, history, and politics is enriched and humanized when these subjects are taught with an eye on the drama of human life upon this earth. The more mechanical subjects come alive when they are put in the context of the living matter of " the human enterprise." " Teaching " is transformed when it is done in and for " life." So also, it cannot but be profoundly influenced by the teacher's recognition that what is going on in himself and in his pupils is not merely " learning," or habit-forming, or exercise, but, fundamental to all these, the conversion of sinners, the reconciliation of people to God, deliverance from bondage to sin and death into the freedom wherein we love our God as our God and our neighbor as ourselves.

## Some Common Pitfalls

Traditional education has been dominated by the notion of transmitting knowledge. Progressive and experimentalist education has

sought to foster the development of the learner through actual experience with situations and problems. The former has been more
emphatic on discipline and factual knowledge; the latter, on freedom and the proper use of knowledge for growth. But both have
been, even when conducted in religious institutions, " secular." By
secular I mean without regard to the spirit of a human being, to the
workings of "sin and death" as a profound, all-informing, all-
deforming, prevailingly consequential factor in a person's life — in
his mind as well as his body. A perusal of recent writings on education, e.g., *Modern Philosophies and Education,* the last yearbook
of the National Society for the Study of Education, makes it clear
that the writers, in spite of their different philosophical and religious
perspectives, agree on considering the problem of "sin and death,"
which is the problem of man, according to the Pauline and Reformed Protestant theology, as irrelevant to the questions of the
aims and process of education. To these writers, as I think to the
overwhelming majority of our educators, in public or private, in
sectarian or nonsectarian schools, the condition of man which led
God the Father to send his Son into the world for the restoration of
man to his original integrity, for which end the Son of Man " suffered under Pontius Pilate, was crucified, dead, and buried; . . .
the third day . . . rose again " — the condition of man as we know
it through the gospel — has no bearing upon the theory and practice
of education! Now such a " secular " position is, from our point of
view, at best superficial and abstract, and at worst a grand falsehood
which cannot but produce miseducation and frustration for the individual and for the community.

## Man as Mind and Body

The traditional treatment of a human being as mind and body, or
even as an organism in a natural environment, requires criticism —
especially when the mind is conceived as occupied with ideas of
things and the body is conceived as an organism. Such an understanding of man in no way does justice to humanity as we find it in
the person and the work of Jesus Christ. It is not true, in the light
of the gospel, that the crucial and decisive relationship of a human

being is to "nature" or even to "society." There is no good or fruition derived from or dependent upon nature and society which does in fact remove man's anxiety for his life, together with the rebellion, alienation, despair, inhumanity, and death which accompany it. Sin, the mysterious misery of man in the violation of love, or the rejection of the life which is in Christ Jesus, is utterly incongruous with his existence as a being whose business is with nature and society. There is nothing in our give-and-take with the "world" that explains our restiveness as human beings and the power of death which destroys us. A biological and cultural interpretation of "*la misère de l'homme*" is neither logical nor illuminating. Man sins and dies in his relatedness to his fate in the world. He is anxious and foolish because he is related to himself and related to this relation to himself; because in this double relation he is free and responsible to affirm his humanity rather than repudiate it; because when he rejects his humanity, when he curses instead of giving thanks and blessing, he is in the wrong; because he sins against the Father who has made him man, and therewith against himself and his neighbor. Such is the peculiarly human, spiritual dimension of his being. Such is man for whose salvation Christ was crucified and rose from the dead for a new life of freedom and fruition among us. To me, it is unthinkable that any education that aims at man's self-realization, at his integrity and eternal life, should ignore the spirit of man.

### Justification by Intelligence

I think prevailing educational activity in our country is derived from a point of view that is analogous to the doctrine of "justification by works." Our educators want the students to practice certain values like objectivity, integrity, humility, co-operation, tolerance, fairness, and helpfulness. Everyone agrees that such values, or virtues, are good and quite necessary for our way of life. Now, the obvious question is how these excellences are to be realized in the pupils. Everyone agrees that one cannot teach them as one teaches grammar or arithmetic. The traditionalists rely mainly on example and contagion, and the experimentalists rely more on the pupils' "directed" experience. The former depend more upon the teacher's moral maturity or even "greatness," and the latter on the pupils' intelligence. Now I do not deny that there are "great" teachers, although they are admittedly few. But who but a man without sense and without humor would undertake to teach the young under the conviction that he is great enough to do the job? And who educates great teachers? And how is it done? Or is there a pseudoapostolic succession in this matter? Plato had sense enough to know that the teaching of virtue is the trickiest and most hazardous business on earth, and that for every Socrates there is a host of Sophists. No sooner does a man begin to fancy that he is great enough to teach than he becomes a "preceptor." No sooner does a man set himself up as an example and dream that virtue is being transmitted from him to another by contagion, than he becomes a nuisance and a bore. "Good teachers make good pupils" sounds good, but there is no one good but God. No one is a good teacher except as he knows that to be taught is to be converted, and that conversion is the work of God. Man plants and waters, but God gives the increase. We teach as men, as well as we can, as wisely as we can. But God alone teaches, and that by faith. It may be that poor teaching has much to do with pride, and that no one can teach well except as he knows his own poverty and the riches of Jesus Christ. Arrogant academics are the blight of education, and there is nothing to do about it except by the "righteousness of Christ."

The experimentalists are more sensible in this matter than the traditionalists. They are more Socratic, and at their best do not presume to ooze out virtue and work by contagion. But they expect the intelligence of the student to lead him to all virtue. What the moralists could not accomplish with the will, the progressivists expect to do with the intelligence. Now, just as the free-willers produce a lot of conformity which passes for righteousness, so the intelligence-mongers produce a lot of "well-adjusted" people who pass for "good, decent citizens." People are indeed quite intelligent, intelligent enough to know where their bread is buttered, to know how to make friends and influence people, to become devilishly enlightened in their self-interest. I do not deny that most people can be educated by well-directed experience to do those things which will earn for them the approbation of their neighbors. In our "other-directed" culture this is considered sufficient virtue, and usually it works quite well. But is it not foolish to expect that group discussion and activity will produce *human* beings according to Jesus Christ, except in a setting of Christian concern?

### THE TRUE STATUS OF INTELLIGENCE

Here we must face the crucial issue of human intelligence — I would rather say, of intelligence as it operates in human beings. At this late date it should not be necessary to argue that mind, reason, intelligence, understanding are words that signify a human activity, activity by concrete human beings who use their theoretical power, naturally, for certain practical ends. I think the experimentalists are right in emphasizing that we think toward the solution of certain concrete problems. In our culture, especially, where the scientific method and technological activity predominate, serious thinking has to do with the solution of physical and social problems. Moreover, people tackle these problems, not as mere minds, but as human beings who are concerned with their security, power, and prosperity. Their intelligence expresses itself largely as technical competence, scientific skill, and prudence. Hence their intelligence is clearly instrumental. They try to learn "the order and connection of things" in order that they may accomplish the greatest amount of good. Whitehead is, I think, a truly modern philosopher in his insistence, in *The Aims of Education,* that "education should turn out the pupil with something he knows well and something he can do well." "The insistence in the Platonic culture on disinterested intellectual appreciation is a psychological error. Action and our implication in the transition of events amid the inevitable bond of cause to effect are fundamental" (pp. 58, 57). The intellect that ends in "contemplation" is a cultural anachronism, and it is a psychological anomaly.

Well, then, the theoretical mind is an abstraction. It is the mind of a person with his passions, motives, fears, hopes, and purposes. It is the means of solving some human problem, and its use depends not only on the problem (as the experimentalists would have

it) but also on the person who is using it. When education is concerned with the remaking of human beings, the personal and social
setting of thought becomes a crucial matter. You cannot divorce the
condition of man as anxious and restive — not to say, in " bondage to
sin and death " — from the use he makes of his mind. Or, to be more
clear, thought is the functioning of a total person, and the mind
shares " the misery of man." An anxious man does not think as
though he were not anxious; a sinner does not argue as though he
were an angel. The intelligence is not only at the service of a problem but also of the man who has the problem. Its solution is not by
the mind but by the man according to his total passion, motive, and
purpose. It is absurd to expect the mind to arrive at justice and truth
unless in the process there is a total reorientation of the person. The
mind must be converted with the man, and this conversion, even
while the mind labors, is not its work but, as Socrates says, a " divine
portion or allotment." No man who has lost himself and found himself anew is in a position to credit his intelligence with his good
fortune. No man who, though having rejected Christ, is embraced
by him credits his intelligence with his new life. The intelligence is
liberated with the rest of a man, and even while active in the liberation, it is not the Teacher.

The notion that the intelligence enables a man to live in integrity,
humility, and love, in fact obscures man's true dignity as a free and
responsible being. There is a subtlety to right action that is lost
sight of in the experimentalist scheme. The mind as such does not
act: the man acts. The man acts by a decision, and then by a " leap."
The mind illumines the situation and so is indispensable, but also,
being in process of conversion, it shares the resistance of the man to
the Teacher. The man must act not only in the light shed by his
mind but also in another light which he sees in the face of Jesus
Christ. He is moved by the Spirit of God, who convicts him of sin
and folly and comes to him with the mercy and wisdom of God. He
is impelled by this same Spirit to decide against himself with his
mind, and in this decision he acts as a free person with a free mind.
He does not follow the insight and prudence of his mind, any more
than he follows the impulse of sin and death in him. He denies him-

self, and consents to Christ. But in this act he acts with his *original* intelligence as a human being. Intelligent action which is essential to humanity is a concomitant of conversion. Without conversion the mind is not capable of solving human problems, because the mind itself creates the problems and its very life is toward death and the sin which goes with it.

The point is that the mind-body pattern, which has dominated traditional education, and the organism-intelligence pattern, which has dominated "progressive education," are much too simple, abstract, and one-sided. They do no justice to the Socratic understanding of the mystery of education; and they lack the Christian understanding of the educational process as one into which God and man, conversion and fulfillment, enter in a profound and fruitful way.

I agree that since man is God's "intelligent creation" (Jonathan Edwards), education that does not issue in intelligence is a farce and a folly. In fact, I should like to insist upon this essential function of education against those pious souls who think that "moral and religious training" is more their business than the training of the mind for integrity and creativity. What we get through such a misunderstanding is poor schools which cater to a timid clientele and produce citizens who are "solid" but not too free or creative. "Creative intelligence" is a glory without which the face of man is dull as a cement wall and the whole of him is a foretaste of death. On this score our Christian colleges must make no compromises and must seek to excel with all others. But unless the former see "creative intelligence" as a fruit of conversion and the work of God in Christ by the Spirit, involving liberation, forgiveness, and a newness of life, they will have nothing of significance to contribute to the educational enterprise.

## THE PROCESS OF EDUCATION

Let us look a little more closely at the educational process in the light of the above considerations. What difference does a Christian theory of education make in the way teachers teach and pupils learn? If God is the Teacher, what, then, is the human teacher doing? What is the pupil doing? And what is the significance of a school or college where teachers and students come together for education?

I would in no wise minimize the importance of the transmission of knowledge. This basic educational activity cannot be slighted without tremendous and even decisive loss not only for the pupil but also for the whole of society and its culture. The scientific, aesthetic, moral, political tradition has to be learned, together with mathematics, language, and history, which are essential for a proper grasp of the tradition. Here knowledge in terms of information and competence in terms of method, skill, and wisdom are essential. But we all know that the *way* one teaches these several subjects makes a great deal of difference, and so does the way the pupils learn. It is always necessary to look beyond a given subject or discipline; and what one sees beyond makes a great deal of difference with what one teaches or learns. What one teaches or learns must be " meaningful," that is, it must contribute to some good. It must be a means, and in being a means it must also be an end: it must have its own intrinsic interest. One must enjoy teaching and learning, and enjoyment goes with the hope that one is " getting someplace."

## HUMILITY IN EDUCATION

When it comes to " the look beyond," the teacher must know his place. Here is where the Socratic or dialectical method of teaching and the modern experimental method come to their own. Both the teacher and the pupil must recognize the prime virtue of humility, the value of exploration, tentativeness, and a free give-and-take in the educational process. I should like to suggest that one contribution of Christian teaching in this instance should be an adequate understanding of humility. Everyone knows we should be humble, but if Socrates is a good instance of humility, we have to admit that it is an extremely rare virtue, not only as an inner disposition but also in practice. Socratic humility and Socratic dialectics go together, and one should not claim the former unless one practices the latter. A teacher who lectures all the time is not likely to be a humble man no matter how he feels.

Socrates is taken to be a rare man. Not every " liberal " or " experimentalist " is a humble man. We Christians should know that humility is at once our despair and our hope. To be humble, a man must be thankful, repentant, and hopeful in Christ Jesus. One can hardly be humble in bondage to sin and death. Humility and freedom, respect for others, equality with others (Kierkegaard), which go with humility, are gifts of God both in the teacher and in the pupil, gifts we receive in Christ Jesus. To the secularist " humility " seems hardly a problem. He fancies himself practicing it left and right. " Let teachers be humble," he says, and there the matter ends. We Christians should know better. Humility is neither a virtue nor a habit. A Christian does not know that he possesses humility. He does not know that he could be humble if he tried to be. He hopes for humility by cleaving to Jesus Christ, under the full power of God who was in Christ reconciling us to himself, to ourselves, and to our fellow men. Humility is in fact a miracle, in one respect the whole of the new life we have in Christ. A Christian teacher exercises humility as an act of faith, by constant recourse to *his* Teacher. When he does this, he receives God's forgiveness and blessing, and true education becomes a genuine possibility. True humility in a teacher is a gift of God, and so therefore is his ability to teach.

## THE LOVE OF TRUTH

Take the matter that a teacher must be a lover of truth. He must be " objective," willing to let truth be realized in himself and in the pupil. Now we all love the truth. No one, no decent teacher, will espouse lies. This is the essence not only of " liberalism " but of all education with integrity. But " truth " is not merely a theoretical matter. A man must live the truth. He must be faithful to the truth. He must practice truth with his neighbor, the teacher with his pupil. To be faithful is to love, for love is what one owes to his neighbor — love that shall make us equals, the teacher with the pupil. The teacher-pupil relationship is human relationship, and in it truth is love, faithful love. One sometimes wishes love had nothing to do with truth. One often protests that one loves as much as the rascals deserve. But a Christian teacher cannot excuse himself so easily. He is to exercise truth by loving his pupils as himself. So and only so it is that he can be their teacher. Once again we have a great difficulty indeed, and it cannot be removed but by the truth or faithfulness of God in Christ toward us.

## INTERESTING EDUCATION

A good teacher, we say, brings his subject alive, arouses the interest of his pupils and keeps it alive. But how are people interested unless they are expectant? And what do they expect which will keep their interest alive? What is really interesting, and where is interest authentic rather than artificial or sentimental? Can a healthy human being be and remain interested in something that is not his fulfillment as a human being? Can one be interested in language, or art, or science, or history, without the hope that he will be rewarded with a proper exercise of his powers as a human being? In all true education there is the implicit promise of the pupil's joy in a full exercise of his powers, of life fulfilled and death overcome. The only ultimately interesting question is, " Good Teacher, what must I do to inherit eternal life? " Human interest remains alive and life itself remains interesting so long as teacher and pupil, man and his neighbor, ask this question, knowing that it is their common question and the question in all matters that interest them. Any subject becomes intrinsically interesting when it raises (by a common if unspoken understanding) this same question. A teacher is good as a teacher of human beings when, as he teaches, the question arises and stays arisen. But then, the teacher is not foolish enough to think he will answer it. The pupils must not for long be foolish enough to expect the teacher to answer it or to think that science, or literature, or history, or politics will answer it, even though these subjects constantly pose the question and are interesting as such. So what are interesting teachers and interested pupils doing with all the creations of human life and mind but thinking and acting with hope? But where is the hope? In the teacher? In the pupil? In the products of culture? Indeed no. It is in the Teacher who gives eternal life, in God " who kills and brings to life."

In short, we Christians ought to see that education for life, with the concern, creativity, and fulfillment it entails, is a " divine portion and allotment " in Christ Jesus. From such is a Christian theory

of education, and from its practice must grow the contribution of
the Protestant Christian schools to the educational enterprise in our
culture.

## PROCEDURE IN TEACHING

It is not wise to tie up Christian teaching with any school of education, as it is unwise to tie up the Church with any political party.
Still, I think the Socratic-dialectic method, which emphasizes the
midwifelike role of the teacher is the one most adaptable to education according to the thesis of this paper. In this method, and the
method of progressive education, it is recognized that the pupil is
taught, not by "the master," but by a Teacher other than man.
Therefore Christian and experimentalist education agree one with
another in their opposition to the notion that the teacher is the prime
actor in teaching. Christian educators should think twice before
they reject the progressive method and advocate traditional, indoctrinating, and moralistic methods.

The Socratic method is related to the Christian in a more positive
way in its insistence that virtue is acquired neither by teaching nor
by exercise, in its methodical humility and its dialectical method. But
Socrates reveled in the dialectical process and obscured "the divine
portion and allotment." I think Christian education should involve
a new dimension in humility as found in Jesus Christ and the new
life in him. Perhaps the dialectical method should be qualified so
that the pupil does not fall into the trap of thinking his reason is
the chief cause of his education. Kierkegaard, whose *Philosophical
Fragments* should be studied most seriously by Christian educators,
made use of parables and an "indirect communication" which go
well with the Christian teacher's dependence upon God for the
conversion of the student. I think that one should encourage the
pupil to argue as clearly and cogently as possible, and that there
should be no letdown in dialectics due to indolence or false piety.
Still, I think one should alternate dialectics with silence. One should
always be ready for light that comes as a surprise. One should be profoundly passive as well as active. One should be tentative, ready to
turn around and go in another direction, lured by hope and encouraged by faith in Jesus Christ. When we consider how the mind

of Christ is an offense, and how we are prone to argue ourselves away from it, we are driven to be critical of our very dialectic even while we pursue it with the knowledge that God converts the mind by the Spirit. We are constrained to add to the dialectical and doctrinaire methods one which we might call the invocative method, in which we exercise the prime privilege of the Christian, which is to call on God (Calvin). I do not mean that we should turn the classroom into a meeting place for formal praying. I mean, rather, that education should involve an expectancy for conversion, which is the prime concern of a Christian. Such expectancy cannot, of course, be turned into a " method." But it can find expression in common " standing still," in a sense of common quest and openness, in a give-and-take among the learners including the teacher, in physical and verbal signs, which show that our business is with God, and therefore spiritual. So Christian teaching and learning become a confession of faith, and there is no doubt that God alone is our Teacher.

## MAN'S BUSINESS IS WITH GOD

But there is to be no compromise in the business of becoming competent and cultivated. We have to know mathematics, language, science, art, politics, and the rest. We are to understand what is going on. Since much of what we study is cultural, and since culture is the work of God in the human spirit, we are to understand literature, history, economics, sociology as expressions of the give-and-take between God and man and therewith among men. And since science and technology are intricately involved with the life of man (Whitehead), even here to ignore the spirit of man persistently is bound to have dreadful results in the education of man. There is nothing more incongruous and defeating in a Christian school than that the sciences, and especially the humanities, should be taught as though man's last business were not with God. There is such a thing as a Christian understanding of *Hamlet* and *Moby Dick,* of Mozart and Cézanne; of Adam Smith and Karl Marx; of Greek history and American politics; of anxiety and social disintegration; and even of the place of industry and agriculture in a human community. Where should such understandings be cultivated if not in a Christian school, in a Christian community of thinkers and learners? Of course, the Christian point of view is not the only one. One must even allow for different points of view and opportunity for serious discussion among Christian educators. Our pluralistic society, I hope, will never allow itself to be bound to any one interpretation of culture. Still, if a school calls itself Christian and if the faculty of such a school believe in Christ as the wisdom and power of God, yea, in the cross as the redemption of man and therewith of the total life of man, then I do not see how it can escape its responsibility, its most grave responsibility, to God, man and country, for making its own indispensable contribution to the total educational enterprise.

It seems to me to follow that teachers in a Christian school should be Christians, without the least compromise with regard to their professional competence. Teachers in a Protestant school should be Protestants. I have, as it were, "the willies" when I say this, because I am aware that a school cannot be vigorous without the stimulation of different points of view. But our present problem is the one of having schools that will make a proper Christian contribution to education. I think they might well include a number of heretics and others. Besides, in a Protestant college there will be much discussion as to what, after all, constitutes a Christian point of view. Moreover, the doors of such a college must always be open to proponents of every kind of point of view, and the better they are, the more welcome they should be. Still, a Christian school that does not work with a Christian understanding of the human enterprise, with the person and work of Christ as its life and energy, that does not engage in the process of education as informed and quickened by the Teacher who is the Spirit of the Father in the Son, is salt without savor and deserves to be thrown away by the Church and forgotten by the people.

## THE STATE AND CHRISTIAN EDUCATION

I must say a word about the State and Christian education. In our society, the State cannot establish and maintain "Protestant schools" in our sense of the term. But it is important that our

Government understand the functions of these schools and afford them such recognition and encouragement as will increase their usefulness in the community. It should take a similar attitude toward Catholic and Jewish schools, as well as " privately endowed " schools that work with clearly valid educational ideals. I am not competent to judge on all the issues involved in the controversy with regard to State aid to non-State schools. But I do think that it is not to the advantage of the people of this land that schools that might make a vital contribution to the total educational enterprise should suffer under peculiar handicaps. A Christian school, provided it is a Christian school, deserves as much support as any other kind of school. But under our political circumstances, it is best that such support come from Christians, both apart from and under ecclesiastical government. In any case, it is never worth-while to sacrifice " academic freedom." A Christian college needs to be in a position to exercise a new freedom, one which is " more than " the freedom of secular schools. But this is one of the many considerations that cannot be undertaken at this time.

I must warn you that nothing is to be gained, and much is to be lost, by a " Christian education " that consists in indoctrination, aimed at the making of decent, docile, dull, and disgruntled youth such as one finds on pious campuses. It is quite possible, and perhaps common, to teach " the Christian religion " in terms of words that have no living significance. To tell the young that since we are Christians we must believe this or that is to cultivate credulity, docility, and lack of reflection and freedom, which are detrimental to education for human fruition. " Christian " schools have suffered from this kind of thing long enough. " Sound doctrine " and " good morals " are not sufficient to make a Christian *school*. When they are made the reason for the existence of " religious " schools, these latter become inevitably second-rate and prevent rather than perform education.

Christian schools must educate better and not worse than secular schools. They must be able to do so because of an understanding (when they have it) of the educational process based upon the truth of our humanity which is in Christ Jesus, because their teachers understand man as a spirit, and because they "teach" accordingly. Unless Christian educators understand the difference between the Christian view of man and the secular, unless they know the difference between the goodness that is in Christ and what men call virtues and values, unless they have a view of teaching that understands that God in Christ and the Spirit alone is the Teacher, unless the whole life of the Christian school, as well as formal teaching, is informed by the gospel — there is no need to be obsessed with the idea of a Christian college.

To put the matter positively: the Christian understanding of human life as a restoration to humanity in Jesus Christ, by the Spirit of God working among us, requires that the Christian people make their peculiar contribution to the task of education in our land, a contribution which is, according to our faith, indispensable for a good society of human beings.

# 3

## FAITH AND REASON
### J. Edward Dirks

THE challenge to define the Christian foundations, in the heritage of the Protestant Reformation, that can support the meaning and task of education in our time demands that we give our attention to the difficult problem posed by the relation of faith and reason. It is a problem which takes us directly into a consideration of the nature and foundations of human knowledge. And nothing else can have a prior place for our colleges and universities, since it is their high vocation to engage persons who search for knowledge and who communicate and apply it in our common life in the world.

### THE SCOPE OF THE PROBLEM

The problem of faith and reason is, however, not merely an academic question. It has its inescapable cultural dimensions. We live in a time when the cultural situation is strikingly similar to that of the Middle Ages when the universities were born. Then it was the intellectual thrust of an Aristotelian naturalism and rationalism that was hostile to the essentially Christian substance of Western culture. Today it is the presuppositions hostile to Christian faith and life that are shaping the context of our culture, which, moreover, is involved in crisis — in part because the medieval Thomistic response to Aristotelian philosophy exacted the high price of splitting between the head and the heart, between reason and faith. By the perpetuation of this tragic separation and in the absence of a distinctly Christian solution restoring their mutual interrelationships, the field has been left open to scientific naturalism and humanistic rationalism to develop an epistemology which excludes the concerns of faith from the realms of rational inquiry. The Christian community, especially as it is expressed in the areas of education, cannot be indifferent to the results of the disjuncture between faith and reason; it cannot ignore the cultural situation in which faith, both as belief and as trust, is implicitly denied. The encounter with culture, therefore, demands a thorough exploration of how reason may be employed, both in its own realms of critical inquiry and with respect to the cause of faith in the midst of a hostile world.

Our colleges and universities have as their task the training of society's leaders, the orientation of each new generation into the common storehouses of human knowledge, the constant examination of the materials of learning for the meeting of contemporary needs, and the transmission and transformation of all the means by which men seek to be and to stay human. Yet institutions of higher education can serve only in their own distinctive way, that is, by employing the disciplines of knowledge for the guided, rational quest of truth. Thus at the cultural level, we find that nearly the whole of man's energies are being used, in the name of reason, for " the practice of the *absence* of God," as someone has defined secularism. An appeal to reason is demanded if we would articulate the meaning and the implications of Christian faith in our time. The task of evangelism has as its premise the acknowledgment by Christians that they are " in the world, but not of it."

### THE APPROACHES TO THE SOLUTION

A historical review of the problem of faith and reason would bring into sharp relief the several major alternatives which are proposed as the solution to the problem. At least three different approaches can be clearly delineated. If we examine these briefly, we can more adequately describe a meaningful Christian view of their relationship.

The first of these approaches views faith and reason as wholly distinct, and even as contradictory, ways of knowledge. The strict Aristotelian of the thirteenth century, the optimistic humanist of

the nineteenth century, and the disciple of positivism or scientism
in our own time hold to this approach. Faith is associated with
either superstition or guesswork; it is composed of long-range hopes
accepted by an act of will contrary to reason, or of propositions that
have behind them the authority of divine revelation. Faith, in this
view, deals with what is unproved, and, hence, unimportant, while
science, which is based on clear rational proof and empirical evidence,
is trustworthy knowledge. On the opposite side there are those who
insist upon the same bifurcation because faith alone has ultimate
priority, while reason vainly seeks for ultimate truth. Tertullian
passionately asked: " What is there in common between Athens
and Jerusalem? What, between the Academy and the Church? . . .
Away with all projects for a ' Stoic,' a ' Platonic,' or a ' Dialectic '
Christianity." In a still more famous passage, he says: " The Son of
God was born — I am not ashamed of it because it is shameful; the
Son of God died — it is credible for the very reason that it is silly;
and, having been buried, he rose again — it is certain because it is
impossible."

In the modern period, we can refer to two writers, one of whom
holds reason as superior while the other maintains a priority for
faith, who reveal the sharp separation that is maintained between
faith and reason. W. T. Stace, the contemporary philosopher, finds
complete contradiction between a " religious view of the world "
and a " scientific or naturalistic view of the world." Religious dogmas
are essentially myths and images, devoid of cognitive content; they
hint at the highly selective experience of the saint or the mystic.
Their " truth " is consequently of a highly subjective order, for it is
contained within a frame of reference for which God alone is real
and the world is illusion. At the other extreme is the naturalistic
view of the world which is labeled " objective," and for which God
is illusion and only the world is real. Thus, naturalism is true of the
natural order; and mysticism is true of the subjective order. They
are vastly separated and cannot interfere with one another or be
found in conflict. A similar approach, based on theological premises,
is followed most clearly by Nicolas Berdyaev. Religious truth is
wholly revelational and is entirely devoid of all cognition. Reason,

on the other hand, deals with cognitive knowledge. The only con-flicts between them develop as theology becomes a social phenome-non and forces reason's subjection to its dogmas; or as " science," in the name of reason, expresses the jealousy that arises out of hostility to what is set forth as revelational " knowledge." In any event, faith is reserved for pure revelation, the essence of religion, while reason has a justifiable claim to all degrees of cognitive knowledge.

So to separate faith and reason creates a tragic dualism both for the modes of human knowledge and for man himself. It is espe-cially perilous for education. It precludes access to the full range of knowledge which is relevant to the whole of man's life, for it de-mands a split between the cognitive and the affective or volitional impulses of man's quest for knowledge. When institutions of higher education assent to this point of view — as most of them do — they may actually contribute to the anti-intellectualism prevalent even in a society which continues to give a prominent role to education. By excluding from education the values of Christian motives and in-sights, and by effecting a sharp bifurcation between faith and rea-son, we eliminate every way of relating the perspectives of faith to the disciplines of knowledge. Then the call to a Christian vocation in scholarship will not be meaningful. And, at the same time, the various academic disciplines remain in their fragmented state of separation and cannot be related to one another in a purposeful quest for truth itself. In this view no common foundation exists for truth, and we have a perpetuation of the old notion of a double truth.

The second of the historical approaches to the relation of faith and reason retains a distinction between their functions while it relates them in terms of their common object. This view found its classical expression in the Thomistic synthesis. It is an apologetical approach, for it seeks to show that while faith and reason are dis-tinct in their modes of operation, and even in their content, they are, in actuality only opposite sides of the same coin. Reason is con-ceived as a natural endowment, uncorrupted by sin, and capable of comprehending all of natural knowledge. Reason develops its own rational principles as it relates itself to the empirical materials of the natural world. Reason, then, is demonstrative; but it has its limits — by virtue of the fact that there is more to be known than the natural world offers. Thus reason cannot carry human knowledge to the supernatural levels of knowledge. Here faith is called upon, as the means of knowledge whereby divine revelation — conceived of as ultimate truth in the form of rationally constructed propositions — is accepted. The knowledge which is received by faith is, therefore, also rational, though its foundations are not in the natural world but in revelation. The position is well summarized in Thomas Aquinas' own words, as follows:

> " The truth of the intelligible things of God is twofold, one to which the inquiry of reason can attain, the other which surpasses the whole range of human reason; both are fittingly proposed by God to man as an object of belief. We must show this with regard to that truth which is attainable by the inquiry of reason, lest it appears to some, that since it can be attained by reason, it was useless to make it an object of faith by supernatural inspiration. . . . (There are disadvantages which result if this truth were left solely to the inquiry of reason.) Accordingly, the divine clemency has made this salutary commandment, that even some things that reason is able to investigate must be held by faith; so that all may share in the knowledge of God easily, and without doubt or error."

This view retains a sharp distinction between faith and reason, but instead of being viewed as in conflict, they are different modes of knowledge focused upon the same intelligible object. They are at the same time sharply distinguished and closely allied. " Natural reason cannot be opposed to the truth of faith " is Thomas' reiterated claim in his descriptions of the arguments for the existence of God. Since Christian beliefs are a total unity, and since some at least can be shown to be available also to natural reason, Thomas claims that all which faith knows is also in accord with reason. Faith is intellectual assent to rational ideas derived from supernatural revelation. Reason is the competent human instrument for all natural knowledge, and, in its farthest reaches, it is the prelude to faith itself.

From the standpoint of educational philosophy, this approach leaves us with a dual-storied structure of knowledge, the whole foundation of which is built by reason, and the additional materials of which are supplied by faith. A bifurcation of knowledge continues, and the disciplines of the arts and sciences are encouraged to proceed on rational premises in accordance with the propositions which are derived from revelation. The cause of Christian faith in relation to knowledge is, therefore, acknowledged only in the upper reaches where supplemental knowledge is added by faith, or as it has the function of laying cognitive foundations for the structures of knowledge. A theory of education built on this view is invariably committed to making theology the a priori cornerstone on which the other disciplines rest, or of seeking to restore it to the role as queen of the sciences. In either event we have a philosophy of education that not only flies in the face of the modern revolt against authority but also, in the name of faith, endorses a pseudorationalism and perpetuates a division between reason and faith which is an injustice to both.

The third of the historical approaches to this problem is the oldest and most perennial of them all. It emerged in its earliest form as the first century Christian Church devoted itself to the proclamation of its gospel in the world of Hellenistic culture. The intellectual climate was saturated by two currents of thought. One consisted of the ethicomystical philosophies which had been grown in Greek soil and which offered either a welcome way of escape from, or a reasonably endurable way of living in, the ordered, boring, and apparently limitless existence under Roman administration, occupation, and taxation. The other current of thought was an inclusive world view, the furniture of which was provided by Greek concepts. There was room for serene ideas, not for empirical things; history was viewed as circular, bent upon harmony and order, but denying meaning to singular events which determined history's purposes; man was viewed as a dualism of body and mind or spirit, in which the corporeal was identified with the tangible and illusory and in which the soul was viewed as eternal; and the divine consisted of a distantly apprehended deity uninvolved in and unconcerned about the affairs of men and this world.

Hellenism, with its sense of despair and futility, provided the background of the early proclamation of a gospel that gave its central attention to the fact of human sin, the event of Jesus the Christ and his life, death, and resurrection, and the offer of redemption by God in Christ, reconciling all men, Gentile and Jew, slave and free, to himself. Christianity offered deliverance beyond anything promised by the Hellenistic philosophies; it insisted that the Christian claim, " Jesus Christ is Lord," had full relevance for a world in which it was required that men claim Caesar as Lord; it centered in Jesus Christ, who was God in the midst of men; who suffered, died, and was raised to new life in order that men, both in this world and in the next, might know the glory of a relationship with God the Father. Instead of peaceful harmony, the Christians bore witness to a conflict between God and the powers of darkness which gave the cross both its grim and its triumphant meaning. They claimed that concrete reality, in its singular and personal form, is the most real of all, not the serene and placid ideas in a heaven of eternal forms. They insisted that history is meaningful because it has a beginning and an end, and for their evidence they pointed to its center, Jesus Christ.

As the message of Christian gospel engaged in battle with the intellectual thrusts of Hellenism, an explosion occurred which was revolutionary for the whole history of human knowledge. There were times when, like Tertullian, Christians washed their hands of Hellenistic culture. Almost in despair, Paul cried out: " Where is the wise? . . . where is the disputer of this world? " (I Cor.1:20). But, in more profound and penetrating moments (as in his Letter to the Ephesians), Paul could interpret the gospel as the final unraveling of a mystery that had baffled the minds of men since the creation. The encounter was between reason and faith, and as the gospel was being proclaimed in a Greek world, a mutual attraction between reason and faith ensued. It was increasingly apparent that God had called the Christian community into such a world as had been shaped by Greek wisdom. The tradition of that wisdom had become sterile, and reason needed the inspiration of new themes which it found in Christianity. And Christianity was being disciplined by the need of understanding the meaning of faith. Faith and reason met as Christian faith wanted to understand itself, and as the tradition of reason wanted something new to understand.

The dialectical approach was given its classical expression in the thought of Saint Augustine. He drew upon all that the unconverted Greek mind could bring to the service of the Church, and he so interpreted the knowledge that was given in revelation that centuries later, when the scientific and speculative impulse asserted itself in the West, there was already a ten-century-old tradition which provided the substantive foundation for scientific procedure. Great names were associated with that tradition — they include Anselm, Bonaventure, and Duns Scotus. Here we find no deprecation of reason, but rather a desire to use it to the full to understand what is known in faith; and without faith reason is impotent because devoid of its material, its themes, and its content, for these have their origin in faith. Moreover, when faith is being shared in a world conditioned by reason, it can be proclaimed only in terms that speak to the probing questions of the rational mind.

## THE THEOLOGICAL RENAISSANCE

It is the distinctive claim of this third approach, especially as it was given its vigorous expression in the Protestant Reformation and as it is being reasserted currently in what is often referred to as " a theological renaissance," that faith is involved in all levels of human experience and knowledge. Likewise, reason is viewed as having the significant task of elaborating and understanding faith's commitments on equally inclusive grounds. Reason can determine the coherency of the perspectives by which man lives; it can establish the criteria which can be employed to make comparative studies of alternative perspectives; it can organize and analyze the data by which the perspectives of faith are relevant. But reason proceeds on a foundation and with material supplied by faith. Thus reason is dependent upon faith. On the other hand, faith is impotent in an understanding of itself, of its relevancy and implications, and of its significance for human life unless it is linked in a partnership with reason so that it may be liberated to break beyond its own and otherwise limited framework. This means, equally, that faith is in some measure dependent upon reason. They are, therefore, linked together in a mutuality, or more accurately in a dialectic, in which each is essential to the other.

I recall that A. D. Lindsay, formerly master of Baliol College, Oxford, once compared the relation of faith and reason to the relation between two lovers who were forced to separate their ways. They were warned, however, that it would be necessary for each to keep the other in mind for his own self-discipline. If reason forgot faith, reason would become, he said, grotesque and brutelike; and, if faith forgot reason then faith would be incapable of retaining firmness and vigor. To be sure, the history of modern epistemology is the story of mutual forgetfulness and even divorce. The cause of reason has been extolled as man's mastery over nature, and his own destiny has been made almost complete. The cause of faith, when it was not seeking refuge from the attacks of modern science, seemed to be engaged in disputing questions no one was seriously asking, or it was asserting its authoritarian claims for an infallible but often unintelligible Bible to a world bent on escaping every authority. However, the tragedy has been on the sides of both reason and faith, and it has engulfed, in addition, a whole culture which has become schizoid.

The tradition of reason in the modern period has moved unrelentlessly toward utter skepticism and nihilism. David Hume and Friedrich Nietzsche are perhaps its best symbols. Knowledge, said Hume, consists in the coherence of ideas, but ideas are based upon distinct and separated perceptions, and the connections between them are made by habit and not by reason or by perceptions. The end result is phenomenalism, which is, in substance, the denial of knowledge. It was this absolute skepticism which aroused Kant to define the limits of reason and to leave us a legacy that separates between the pure and the practical reason. Nietzsche, on the other hand, accepted the nineteenth century shift from a mechanistic to a more organismic interpretation of nature. He found that whatever meaning could be ascribed to existence had its roots in nature itself, defined in the evolutionary theory of natural selection. Applying it to

the realm of morals, he called for a transvaluation of values, an aban-
donment of humility and mutual concern among men, and the
future creation of a race of men who survive and stand supreme in
the struggle for existence.

When the history of modern thought is finally written in the
future, it will undoubtedly be obvious that modern epistemology, in
all the areas of knowledge, is a story of the triumph of naturalism.
Even the traditions of idealism and romanticism, with their deifica-
tions of nature and mind, can be interpreted in this framework. The
whole of reality will be seen as having been viewed within a context of spatiotemporal events, subject to measurement and analysis
by scientific means, and their relations governed by laws that, if
they can be known at all, are elaborated in mechanistic and mathematical terms. The end result will be apparent: a form of reduc-
tionism of all reality to the single plane of nature, the knowledge of
which is limited to the positive sciences. For such a world view —
the total elaboration of all the implications of a universe from which
God has been banished and whose throne is taken by man himself —
the role of faith is without meaning. To be sure, it may continue as
an acceptance of certain transempirical truths which have behind
them the authority of revelation, or it may persist as a moral framework which appears to be needful if man is to go on living. But
its vigor and vitality will have been depleted by the apostasy of
modern civilization.

It is this background that constitutes the challenge to those of us
who are engaged in the enterprise of education, and it is especially
poignant in relation to the problem of faith and reason. We need
desperately to engage all our resources in elaborating a Christian
philosophy of education which can be a healing and redemptive
force for man's total life in our time. Such a philosophy which is at
the same time true to our Christian heritage and adequate to the
inclusive task of education must be large enough to meet the comprehensive dimensions of the crisis of our age. What we are challenged to formulate is a theology of knowledge that can speak to
the whole of human concern, and is adequate to the task of recon-
struction in higher education.

Our fundamental Christian convictions, especially as they are related to knowledge, must once again be reaffirmed and set forth as the foundation upon which such a theology of knowledge can be built. Here the contemporary theological renaissance can give us many helpful resources. We need to take seriously the Christian claim that knowledge is essentially personal and historical, and that at its highest levels it is imparted through self-disclosure, which is the nature of revelation. We need also to remember that man, the subject of knowledge, is created by God to be a responsive being, and that it belongs to his responsiveness to confront himself, his fellow men, the world of nature, and even the Most High God, with the questions that deal with the meaning of his existence, in the light of the Biblical assertion that man is made in the image of God. But we need also to be reminded of the further word about man, the word of judgment, which reveals our sin, the total distortion of our creaturely life, the disruption of our relatedness to ourselves, to others, to the world, and to God. All this is involved in the fall of man. But there is a further word, which speaks of forgiveness and restoration, by the act of being brought into the community of faith which renews the freedom by which the quest of knowledge can move forward. And looking out upon the world and upon history from that community — the redeemed and redemptive community — the man of faith sees it in its totality as dependent upon God. In this knowledge — the knowledge of a contingent order of existence — the deepest sense of mystery is born; and out of mystery, rather than out of the impulse for power, there arise the kinds of questions that stimulate inquiry and the search for knowledge.

Moreover, the kinds of questions that grow from the soil of mystery not only lead us down the isolated private paths of individual search, but also introduce us to the company of those who, throughout the ages, seek to know the truth. We find that we ask the questions with others and we become part of a community engaged in mutual search and inquiry. Even when we fail to get coherent answers, we nevertheless find that we have been joined with the lives of a whole company for whom the desire for knowledge and understanding is the motivating force of their being. Thus, we discover that our approach to truth is a kind of dialogue; it is more like a conversation than the outlining of a system of ideas. As we engage in the quest, we become part of a community of persons, which stimulates, sustains, develops, and in part satisfies our further quest.

## THE COMMUNITY CHARACTER OF EDUCATION

The foundations of a Christian philosophy of education rest on Christian convictions and on the inescapable community character of education itself. The components of such a philosophy must be found in a Christian theology of knowledge which can adequately relate faith and reason. It must meet at least three demands. Let us look at each of them more carefully.

First, such a theology of education must have its center in a Christian view of the nature of faith. Our Protestant Reformers took their departure believing in the Biblical assertion that man is " justified by faith " (Rom. 3:28; 5:1; Gal. 3:24). They were recalling a rich heritage which emphasized both the faithfulness of God and the nature of man's response to the divine gift of salvation. They were insisting that, though man had denied his created destiny, God had acted in Christ in such a way that man could be restored to God, and that man, in his response of faith, could have returned to him his created essence as a child of God. The central emphasis was upon faith, which, as the gift of God, made possible the " new man " in Christ. This was to deny the redemptive efficacy of merely human efforts, legalistic or ritualistic, ethical or intellectual. But, in its positive form, it was an attempt to say that faith is a relationship with God, analogous to the relationships between persons. Its closest synonym is trust, the commitment of one's life in all its aspects to a relatedness of life to God.

Christian thinking proceeds from the fundamental principle that human living involves a commitment — one that is inescapably bent by a primary loyalty or allegiance in which all the constituent aspects of life find their focus. The question which the gospel asks in judgment is always the question of one's life perspective or world view; namely, is this view shaped by the glorification of the living God or by something else which is not worthy of ultimate trust but has perhaps been elevated to the supreme position of the divine? The Christian faith reveals that the conflict of life is between various religious perspectives, not between a religious and an irreligious one. It interprets the tension as between trust in the living God and trust in something else — a social program, human rationality, the order of nature, the authority of the Church — which may assume the center of ultimate loyalty and concern. The Bible constantly impresses upon us the struggle between the true God and the idols of man's own making, and the call of the Bible is always for a return to the true God and a leaving behind of idolatry. The tension is therefore one of opposing faiths, not one between faith and its alternatives.

Here faith is conceived as an inclusive orientation to life, as a perspective by which life is shaped. Thus it is far-reaching as a network of ideas and concerns, for it is the kind of commitment that alters every aspect of our life, including our conceptions and the range of our concerns. Thus faith is a world view, a framework by means of which we understand the order of nature, the patterns of history, as well as the most minute details of the sciences and the arts. Christian faith represents a total change of mind, intellectual and moral, in which the overarching and the underlying commitment is to God, as the true center of human existence. It is a response to God's self-disclosure as the God who can save us by returning us to himself. Thus, Christianity is not speculative; its reality is constituted by the continuous interaction between the living God and a people that accepts his word in faith and seeks to be obedient to it by his grace. The word and the act are thus united both by God in his self-disclosure and by man in his response. Out of this union a people is born, a community is established, and a new life of trust and freedom is created.

But Christian faith finds its opposition and its alternatives in other faiths, in other ways of accounting for our human existence in the world, in other forms of commitment. Man lives by faith and he has only a choice as to the nature of his faith. But this verity also includes human thinking, and thus all branches of knowledge, and all ways of exploring the realms of being, are dependent upon com-

mitments and presuppositions. The assumption of order and regu-
larity in the natural world, the presupposition that what is known
is capable of being expressed and communicated, the acceptance of
the intelligible material to which the mind can be related—all
these derive from commitments, from the foundations of faith. They
are not self-evident propositions; and, they are not established a
posteriori by empirical evidence. They are the kinds of sources of
truth that are needed for the selection of facts, the development of
coherent knowledge, and the application of knowledge to the whole
range of human activity. Without such presuppositions admitting
all truth, the progress which is possible in the sciences, where the
symbols and laws of mathematics are combined with observation and
experiment, would be vitiated. Without them we should not have
history but merely the chronicling of events.

It is the Christian view that there is a distinctive perspective that
derives from, or is constituted by, trust in God. It is a view that
acknowledges God as having complete control of the world and its
natural, historical, and personal events; that his control is exercised in
a purposeful way; and that he communicates the commands and
promises that reveal man's place in his designs. It is a perspective
that finds its fullest expression in Christ, who revealed the nature of
this ultimate commitment by living the life of God in man's midst. It
is the Christian claim that this kind of commitment, as it is shared
in Christ, opens up, not only a new life, but a new range of human
experience and discovery. It gives facts new significance; it gives
rise to new questions and to a distinctive set of theories which help
us in understanding the known facts, while they point the way for
further inquiries.

It is the task of reason to explicate the nature of the commitment,
and to describe its implications as a perspective for all the facts, questions, and theories. Thus, reason works with the materials which are
supplied to it by faith. It serves as the instrument of criticism, as
the means of analysis and sharing the content and implications of
our faith with others. Because faith is closely related to the cognitive enterprise, revelation, upon which faith is established, need not
be regarded as irrational. On the contrary, revelation is the illumina-

tion of the minds of men as the totality of their lives is drawn within the orbit of God's redemptive love.

Thus, both faith and reason have an inclusive role which moves from the most minute items of human experience to the grandest actions of the human drama. Faith has the prior role, yet reason is needed to make faith operative. And reason can become effective only when it is supplied by the material that is given it by faith. The relation is one of reciprocity. Reason contributes as it makes a critical analysis of faith, tests its premises, interrogates its criteria, and holds in check its tendency to resort to authority. Faith depends upon reason, for as reason engages in its work, faith becomes deepened and enlarged.

Secondly, a Christian theology of education must fully recognize the role of reason as the instrument of inquiry. The traditional rationalistic interpretation of reason exalts it as the sole means of deriving ultimate principles and as the means whereby these a priori principles can be utilized in the building of the edifice of knowledge. The philosophy of René Descartes gives us a classical expression of such a view of reason. He held to the view that the exercise of reason is, in effect, the foundation of existence. Thus, as reason derives its own principles, it can build a reliable structure of interrelated concepts which can form a total and inclusive interpretation of reality. But a Christian reading of the history of philosophy reveals that reason's distinctive role is to be found in critical analysis, in probing inquiry, and in determining logical coherency. Reason does not stand out as the groundwork upon which world views or metaphysical systems are built. Under the influence of scientific methods, it is often assumed that a world view is the result of inductive generalizations from a mass of data from various quarters. It is sometimes asserted that the person who develops the world view is a detached spectator who works only as if motivated by a " disinterested curiosity " and whose personal destiny is not involved in the results of his thinking. Such an assertion is an inaccurate description of the process of reason. A world view is not itself a scientific theory, though it may give rise to theories. It is motivated by a desire to see life whole, and it seeks to set forth a perspective of all reality and its meaning.

Various specific differences may be found between various motivations. The scientific naturalist, for example, may only express an interest in the kind of knowledge about the natural world which gives him power for control or exploitation; he links power and knowledge together. The humanistic rationalist, on the other hand, may view knowledge primarily in terms of serene intellectual concepts, the contemplation of which makes the tragic dimensions of existence and the demands for decision in the dynamics of history somewhat easier. But, in either case, the development of a world view takes place as someone thinks outward and forward from a central, dominant acceptance or commitment as he brings all phases of experience into relation with it. This work may be undertaken in the form of a series of pertinent analogies. They supply the links that relate experience and add to its understanding and interpretation. Thus, the world view is, in actuality, constructed by the work of reason and in relation to experience, but always with reference to a central commitment which provides it with dynamics and consistency. Reason's distinctive task is critical elaboration, analysis, and reflection. And it is the function of the college and the university to be a community of rational inquiry. By employing reason in its rightful capacity, the educational community can become a forum in which the various world views are compared and contrasted, where their implications for life and understanding can be traced, and where the various competing perspectives can be brought under the scrutiny and judgment of reason. It is the special role of the Christian college to carry out a rigorous exploration of the relevance of Christian faith to all the fields of inquiry, to all aspects of life, and to all demanding problems of the contemporary world. To do so we must safeguard free inquiry in which the Christian faith is seen in its full relevance and not held in reserve and in which, also, its primary opponents are permitted full expression so that their challenges may be understood. A faith accepted upon critical analysis by reason is better than a faith coddled to avoid contact with reason.

Thirdly, a Christian philosophy of education which recognizes the inclusiveness of faith, and of reason, must also acknowledge the inclusiveness of the impact of human sin. The doctrine of the Fall refers us to a total condition of man. Thomism cut itself off from the Biblical viewpoint by claiming that reason was exempt from the Fall. But the Bible's view of man, through the eyes of faith, interprets sin as changing every aspect of man's life, at all levels. The rebellion against God, which is the essence of sin, has its moral, cognitive, spiritual, social, and individual aspects, all ambiguously interwoven in what is referred to as the loss of the image of God. No function or part of man's life is exempt from the impact and influence of sin.

Thus, the intellect of man is always viewed with ambivalence from the standpoint of Christian faith. The intellect definitively accepts or rejects. Faith involves openness to continued accepting and rejecting. In pride the intellect asserts for itself a larger sovereignty than it can command. To refer to the noetic effects of sin is to underscore particularly the stultifying effects of sin on the intellect. It is, to use Luther's phrase, man turning inward upon himself; it is another form of idolatry, and it is often the idolatry of a human capacity which gives man power, such as reason. But when reason seeks to build an inclusive structure of knowledge on its own defective principles, without recognizing its dependence upon faith, it actually rules out or denies God — and thus his purposes for man — and so fails in its highest possibilities. Moreover, the exercise of reason, even in its own proper sphere, can be used for purposes which distort, and even destroy, faith. Thus faith must be constantly renewed as it encounters the critical movement of reason, which would claim us for itself and separate us from God. However, the Christian who acknowledges the continuing grace of forgiveness and justification has the assurance of the Spirit and the Word in answer to the question, "Who shall separate us from the love of Christ?" (Rom. 8:35) and the Scripture, "Where sin abounded, grace did much more abound" (Rom. 5:20). Thus faith as a concomitant and a corrective of reason is perhaps more needful in the community of inquiry than anywhere else in the life of the Church.

### THE "MEETING" OF FAITH AND REASON

We can summarize our thesis, then, by quoting a phrase which is used widely in contemporary theology. "Christian faith is a meeting." But it is a meeting that takes place where the divine reason (or logos) sets up its law in the region of man's understanding. It is reason's task to discover the implications of this meeting for the whole range of our life and thought; it is by reason that the eyes of faith are helped to see the world, that the voice of faith is helped to say what the eyes see, and that the hands of faith are helped to work for what the voice proclaims. As this happens, knowledge grows and abounds in love. The knowledge is always relative knowledge, for it is forever bound within the limits of the creaturely. But Christian faith has to do with the illumination of reason, and it is by reason that faith grants us the freedom to live and to think in the truth of Jesus Christ. This is a living truth and its knowledge is living knowledge; it is a wisdom that contains knowledge and, insofar as we serve it, becomes the truth which sets us free. Such wisdom is trust in God; it is the meaning of our existence and the ground and goal of all that happens.

The Christian faith is a way of living and a way of dying. But, an understanding of it demands the critical function of reason. To carry both reason and faith into the dynamic realms of human life is the task to which the Christian colleges are called in our era. If they can serve well, they can renew the option of faith for a bewildered age; they can find their own life in the kind of deep commitment that is our highest freedom, and they can rediscover for the Christian community the kind of humility that involves a willingness to stand under the discipline of others' truth. Such service is called for if we would live by the imperatives of our Lord. He calls us to serve him in the campus community; he challenges us to faithfulness and the vigorous task of rational inquiry; and he promises us our perfect freedom. If we can respond to him in his Spirit, we can change our Christian colleges into lighthouses for human civilization in a critical age.

# PART
# II

*Personality*

# 4

## COMMUNITY AND PERSONALITY

### *Theron B. Maxson*

IN ITS most productive thought molds educational philosophy
grows out of the careful examination of the concerns of those
who make up a community. The educator, therefore, is one who
has dedicated himself to a thorough and complete search of all
forces relative to human personality. He reminds himself that the
larger community is held together by broad, general loyalties. He
also is sensitive to the knowledge that smaller segments within the
culture are commonly devoted to specific ideals which they believe
capable of effectively changing the pattern of living for all the people. The teacher is aware of the evidences of history indicating
that periods of crisis have led to distrust in secondary issues and have
generated interest in the reanalysis of assumptions worthy of determining enduring values. He recognizes that threats of conflict
and days of peace call for a note of assurance from some quarter
which can provide the human family with life-sustaining answers.
Some educators are keenly aware that the tenets of the Christian
faith have much to say about loyalties and devotions by which men
learn and live.

The Christian community, as outlined in this chapter, is represented as a distinct fellowship of believers in Jesus Christ as divine
Saviour and Lord of all of life, who not only reveals God to man
but also re-creates personality according to God's plan as expressed
in the writings of the Old and New Testaments. This " fellowship,"
which actively participates in the affairs of men, holds that every
year is a year of critical need as long as any area of life remains

outside the redemptive purposes of God. This concept measures the strength of all forces exerting influence upon the social climate in which Christian education is nurtured. The impact of this fellowship of believers is expressed most effectively through three interrelated agencies: the family, the church, and the school.

## The Complexity of the Social World

The first half of the twentieth century has witnessed unparalleled conquest in the various fields of science through research. Many heretofore uncharted deserts of knowledge have been reduced to symbols understood and freely used even by the high school student. Even so, each new decade seems to push the limit of knowledge farther into the distance. Let it not be forgotten that a complete understanding of objects will mean little without sturdier findings in the relationship of objects to the ultimate nature of man.

New discoveries have brought certain complications. Man's mental and emotional structure has been sorely tried within the tightening proximity of those forces arising from swifter means of communication and transportation. The pressures of his complex social world have increased, and, try as he will to remain objective about truth, he often turns upon himself and resides in the atmosphere of deep introspection. While his creative skills and scientific know-how have skyrocketed, his fears have kept pace. While the healing arts have markedly expanded his life expectancy, and while factual information has destroyed many of the illusions of the " evil spirits " of the ages, the universal problem of understanding himself still faces him, and the elemental concern of his " salvation " — physically, mentally, emotionally, and spiritually — remains paramount. Finding the " abundant life " in any or all of these four spheres is still his foremost quest. Modern man, if he has read the commentary on life by the apostle Paul, has sometimes refused to accept portions of his insight: " And though I have the gift of prophecy, and understand all mysteries, and all knowledge; and though I have all faith, so that I could remove mountains, and have not charity, I am nothing " (I Cor. 13:2). Lost in a maze of informative materials, man sometimes has trouble with the apostle's unifying principle of love; yet, even though frustrated and hard pressed, he still seeks an ultimate goal for himself and for those to whom he is devoted. Scientists, artists, philosophers, and theologians are redoubling their efforts to find ways of relating truths from whatever source. If their motivation is not sheer devotion to truth, it is at least to discover a way out of annihilation, which disaster has so evidently become possible and even probable through reliance on half-truths. For education the discovery of unifying ideas presents a constant challenge. Christian education has an equity here.

## Individuality in a World That Is One

Two pertinent facts have filtered through the mass of words appearing in newspapers and textbooks. The first is that all objects and subjects, despite apparent similarities, have individuality. The second, apparently antithetical to the first, affirms that despite this individuality, life is a complex pattern, both for the person and for his community. The world of men and things cannot be understood in terms of isolated segments. This is the concept of *Gestalt*. Brief examination of these two ideas leads to the rediscovery of an old fact, projected and defined through concept and action in a particular way long ago by those included within the fellowship of the Christian faith. Today we turn for help to the young sciences of psychology and sociology. While these sciences serve to shed light upon the nature of the personality, they have not only shown the uniqueness of the individual but have indicated that in an attempt to preserve the self, man has often destroyed values he has held most dear. Human wastage and nonproductive living have often been observed to be in direct proportion to the use of mechanisms of self-defense. Difficulties related to this fundamental problem have not only persisted through the centuries but have been accentuated in the complex social patterns of the twentieth century.

A number of rather well-ordered schools of psychology have risen in recent decades and have found modifications through further research. The major discoveries of each have contributed something to the knowledge of man. Some investigators have been analytical.

Some have attempted synthesis. Some have given themselves to the study of mental characteristics, the composition of the central and the autonomic nervous system, the role of emotion, the laws of learning and of problem-solving, and to the observation of organic and psychological drives. Others have suggested therapeutic means as a way out of man's maladjustments. Observers in the field of biology — and particularly in genetics — have discovered and disseminated information illustrating nature's method of particularizing life. Each new generation is represented as having unique characteristics. A knowledge of man's yearnings, aspirations, abilities, and social consciousness has been projected through various methodologies into the personnel offices of business and industry, into political campaigns, into the work of the medical center, into psychological warfare, and into the basic institutions of the family, the church, and the school.

Sociology, concerning itself in part with a study of the environment into which the individual is born, has substantiated psychological research in evaluating both the egocentric and the sociocentric patterns within which personality develops. The trend of knowledge in general has been away from atomism toward wholeness. Today the mind of man is attempting perhaps more than in the past to bring together collective information and values from any and all sources in order to give meaning to all of life and in order to save both the individual and the group. The very interdependence of forces at work in the physical and social world seems to fortify the assumption that nothing exists of itself or unto itself. Isolationism in any area seems unworthy of man's intelligence, if it is not downright fantasy and escape. Sometimes man has had to learn this lesson the hard way. Epidemics of fear seem not to be limited by geographical boundaries. Shock waves of anxiety spread to all shores. Physical stress in one part of town can so easily become a pressure for a whole city. Abuse of privilege by a few can limit the freedom for all. As long as there is immorality, or a lessening of the sense of value placed upon the human soul, who is safe? The question answers itself. Hatred and distrust not only destroy the one who hates but also threaten the whole community. Vicious mental commitments cannot be contained within the cells of a single body any more than compassion and sacrifice can be kept from sensitizing the emotions of those concerned. No experience can be confined to the individual self alone. Even the most casual observations suggest that those who teach and those who learn must become increasingly aware of the subsurface forces responsible for many of the breakdowns in human relationships.

Education per se has not provided complete security. Man has discovered that when his spirit is lonely, his days are meaningless and his nights are sleepless. Probably his most cultivated experience is his attempt to find fellowship and harmony with others, but within the very confines of this adventure he is blocked by his own egocentricity. He wants to belong to others, but he does not wish to share his all. Both the child and the man live disturbed lives without communion with another. It has been demonstrated clinically that habits created by this sense of frustration often ripen into one of many forms of personality disorders. The survival of the race therefore calls for continuing research into all the elements responsible for social birth. The final chapter in this development may well be written as a symposium by scientist, theologian, and educator. It is hoped that the real nature of man as a potential child of God will not be forgotten. He must find a larger loyalty outside himself. The Christian community as expressed in the family, the church, and the school must search clear-mindedly and diligently with every means at its command for the whole truth so that it may then speak with a convincing voice.

## EDUCATION IN A DISTINCT COMMUNITY

The trend in research we have mentioned has much to suggest as to the main objectives of this study of the community in which Christian education is nurtured. For even though a Christian considers his citizenship not to be limited by the things he touches, nevertheless much of his sustenance comes from the social milieu in which he lives. Historically, the Christian community has been identified with the organized Church. While its membership cuts across a host of other groups, the fellowship of believers exists as a distinct community. Jesus called this communion in its widest meaning the Kingdom of God and the Kingdom of Heaven. This is a fellowship of God with man and man with God, brought into being through the redemptive purposes of God and serving as a pattern for harmony. The thrust of the Church is expressed through the believer who understands himself to be a child of God. The heart of worship includes personal identification with and commitment to the central, living personality, Jesus Christ as Saviour and Lord. The understanding of this truth so that it will benefit the teaching-learning process centers in one authority — the Holy Scriptures. The nature of God and his program for man's welfare is expressed through his Son, and provides a curriculum as unlimited as the breadth of personality, human and divine. It is only reasonable that such a curriculum would be constantly outgrowing all narrow human devices. It is a curriculum of action. The prime mission of the Church, therefore, is the propagation of truth. Truth alone is able to strike at the heart of the problem of evil and to assure a way of meeting the ultimate needs of man as determined by a fatherly God. This faith creates for the Christian community a sense of belonging in God's universe. Such redemptive processes are erected upon the emotional continuum of love, without which the fellowship of believers would perish, in fact, would never have received birth from God. The fellowship of believers as outlined in the New Testament does not seem to be limited by barriers of time and space or by things. The divine society exists as an institution never to be dissolved, forging an unbroken chain of personal devotion to truth, bridging human generations. Both those " inside " and those " outside " the fellowship are met with the same spirit of love and service since all carry potential as children of God. This circumstance creates a pattern of consistency much needed by the human family and of importance as a working base of operations for the Christian educator.

The very nearness of God to the life of the Church radiates a sense of faith and mission. God's immanence is expressed through the love of Christ and evidenced by his death and resurrection. The Holy Spirit is active in communicating God's will to the Church.

Through the ages the personal nature of divinity has often become dimmed; now through the designs of Christ to "draw all men" unto himself, a new force has entered the affairs of men. Allegiance to this concept has given birth to a powerful educative influence.

These are the expressions of a distinct community within a larger community which has not always recognized the place of God in life. Christian education, therefore, becomes a dynamic process of knowing the whole mind of God, insofar as it is knowable, and relating it to the egocentric personalities that are prone to take incomplete and secondary pathways in searching for fulfillment. The persuasive influence of this "pattern for living" is worthy of exploration by any and all. These are the implications for the community at large, and particularly for the family and the school.

## THE FAMILY AS PRIME EDUCATOR

The first unit of the community is the family. Its power rests within a simple organism held intact by the necessities of love and sharing. The keys to mental stability are here. The home as a classroom must not be underestimated. Not only is its influence the broadest, but its tools are the simplest and its impress the most enduring. The child achieves social birth when he becomes conscious of his interrelationship with another person somewhat like himself. His greatest task is finding maturity within the mold of this idea. It is the crown toward which he grows, and it becomes the most difficult lesson he must learn. Devoid at birth of fears, he soon finds that he has the capacity for fear. As the anxieties of his progenitors spread their unstable wares before him, he learns the hates and prejudices of his small community along with its ideals. He is impressed by the loyalties of those about him. Each loyalty he observes contains an emotional center which soon becomes his property as well as that of his father and his mother. The language he uses, the people he includes, the objects he excludes, the subjects he worships are caught from a host of variable associations. He learns to trade his egocentric pattern for certain securities which only the fellowship of love in the home can provide. He discovers through countless specific experiences that he is independent at times, most dependent at other times. Above everything else he is driven by one major desire — to belong to his father and mother, brothers, sisters, teachers, clubs, schools, church, the world, even the universe, including all personal powers within it. His little world grows into a personalistic cosmos; people mean everything; they give, and they take away. It is in the home that he achieves his first insight into the real nature of man. It is in the home also that he can take the first steps toward understanding something of the nature of God. His insatiable desire to probe the mysteries of the life about him provide motivation for a host of experiences which give to him a meaningful life. The translation of precepts into concepts, of ideas into activities, can through growing commitments condition his ability to inherit and enjoy fellowship in the Kingdom of God and to find deep satisfaction in serving others. The Christian family, therefore, provides not only the setting for reaching biological maturity and the ability to live with other people but also the opportunity to grow through religious experience into an understanding of moral values through spiritual insight.

While authority resides in the household, its cohesive factor is the authority of the concerns of love, and even when stern counsel is in order there is place for forgiveness, redemption, and unity. While individuality is maintained, the home provides a stage for the enactment of the role that sharing can play. Defensiveness gives way to objectivity.

The consciousness of God can be lived overtly by the members of the family. Understanding and practicing this dynamic principle is the parents' primary step in providing Christian education. Devotion to God's purpose is nurtured through worship and service and is deepened through action. Particularized practice assists the child into an understanding of communion with God. The home can allow for the exhibits of God's goodness. It can represent a miniature Kingdom of God. The Christian family does not overlook the spiritual values of deeper devotion; its philosophy is outgoing; its spirit is sacrifice; its tenor transcends the emotional shifts alternating between privation and contentment. The realities of food, shelter, illness, and death are considered as within the concern of the

Heavenly Father as well as that of the family. The problem of guilt and its system of defense, so prominently observed in personality, cannot be side-stepped by educator, theologian, or parent. Counseling, leading to empathy, acts as the norm with the family, resolving feelings of rejection and conflict. Confession and forgiveness are propitious to spiritual growth. Moreover, since they are at the heart of the conversion experience, they provide and foster the idea of fellowship which recognizes that no proclivities in the human being are beyond the understanding and the love of God. The expression of this idea is " lived out " in the family; its magnitude reaches its high peak in the presentation of Christ not only as intimate friend but also as High Priest.

Jesus placed the highest premium upon the importance of the personality of the growing child. " Whoso shall offend one of these little ones which believe in me, it were better for him that a millstone were hanged about his neck, and that he were drowned in the depth of the sea " (Matt. 18:6). Let the educator not forget that a social or spiritual cripple can result when the child is conditioned by those about him in such a way as to prevent the fulfillment of his growing aspirations in a world of man and God. Defenses set up within the center of his nature may prevent his ultimate maturity. Thus the Christian home carries the major responsibility of education, for here it is that the pattern for development is begun. In an attempt to set up worthy goals, the school must exercise care not to erect its curriculum without consideration of the place of the home as an educational center.

### Educational Philosophy and Christian Fellowship

Education within the classroom has been closely allied with that of the home and the church throughout much of the Christian Era. Not only were the apostles teachers, but the Church was still young when catechetical classes helped to prepare the convert for full participation in the ritual and the doctrines of the ecclesia. Famous teaching centers soon sprang up notably in North Africa and southern Europe. Scholars drew heavily upon the Hebrew and the Grecian classics, discovering means of explaining Christian theology through the semantics of philosophy. This teaching ministry, during the first five or six centuries A.D., became far-reaching in its influence.

After Saint Augustine's day there was a growing distrust of the philosophic mind of Greece of the pre-Christian era. In an attempt to preserve an ecclesiastical authority, the educative practices became so narrowed that the psychological needs of the believer were almost forgotten. Religion and life were often divorced. Formalism ran the danger of destroying much of the attitude of devotion of man to man, which had been the magnetic factor of the earlier evangel. A pessimism within the fellowship grew in part out of the dialectic method and reached a climax in Scholasticism. However the Renaissance and the Reformation re-enunciated theology in terms able to cope with the practical problems of the community.

The declarations of Luther, Melanchthon, Calvin, and other thinkers of the centuries immediately following, provided a laboratory of ideas in which to grow educational procedures. An emphasis on Biblical literature in the vernacular plus a new sensitization to literature outside the Bible led to a broader set of teachings within the school. Some teachers gave special attention to the real worth of sensory experience. Students were encouraged to examine all truths and to revaluate past interpretations which had sprung from a day of intense intellectual formalism. A resurgence of interest in the arts and sciences during the Renaissance provided ample material with which the educator could experiment. A world of appreciations through touch, sound, and vision was coming into its own. An essential dualism of object and spirit became woven into the fabric of educational philosophy as a means of nurturing the fellowship of believers. Writings began to appear on the purpose of education as a means of enjoying God's world through better understanding of the pupil and an ever-enlarging curriculum.

By the beginning of the twentieth century numerous philosophical systems had taken root in the Western world. Several were to become distinctly allied with education and were to have far-reaching influence upon the school. Some philosophers premised the reduction of the individual to his simplest observable components; others not only admitted the creative transcendent character of God but allowed for an appraisal of human life through emphasis upon theism.

Christian education during the past fifty years has been caught in the cross fire of many philosophical positions, ranging from the holdings of naturalism and pragmatism to a re-emphasis of idealism in various forms. As the natural sciences have come into their own, man has allied himself each year more definitely with the phenomena of nature. Naturalism, as a result, has provided many important leads to the understanding of the developmental processes of the student within the school. However, education in many quarters has drifted toward an interpretation of man as living in a universe conceived to be quite impersonal. This simple monism causes conflict in the mind of the Christian community. To the fellowship of believers the whole field of knowledge is not limited to such oversimplification; therefore, pure naturalism is considered to be incomplete in its explanation of the personality and of the forces which play upon it. Man is endowed with a spirit as well as with a body, and can relate that spirit intimately to God. The subjectivity of rational man and his self-consciousness demands a metaphysic which, while not limiting the field of sense perception, is not limited by it.

Pragmatism, as applied to education, has made a worthy attempt to rid the educative process of a pure mentalistic formalism, which often in the past had divorced specific life experiences from classroom procedures. Pragmatism's strength lies in its attempt to make education life-centered, using a changing social environment as the basis for continuous reorganization of all experience. Its weakness for the Christian community lies in its lack of ultimate objectives and its suspicion of fixed truth, which is so important to the " fellowship." Believers hold that productive living demands wider horizons than immediate adjustments to changing culture patterns. If personality is to mature through the intervention of the Spirit of God, then there must be co-operation with the permanent laws and purposes of God as ingrained in the very structure of life.

Through these fluctuations in theory Protestantism has sometimes given itself to an eclectic position in educational process. Idealism as an educational philosophy, however, seems to have been consistently prominent in the teaching program of the Church. Those of the

Christian faith find within its framework the insistence upon universal truth as a standard which places before man's mind eternal concepts large enough to change the personality of man as he yearns for the perfection of ideas emanating originally from an all-wise God. This idealism holds to the fundamental mentalistic concept capable of producing enduring values in the mind of the seeker after the truth.

The New Testament assurance of the dwelling of the " mind of Christ " (I Cor. 2:16; cf. Phil. 2:5) within the believer, and his renewal " in the spirit of your mind " (Eph. 4:23), can lead mankind to a comprehension of truth and sound commitments capable of surviving the test of time and tension. This certainty gives permanency of direction to the whole human family. Since all truth is derived from one source, namely, God, and therefore cannot come into conflict, freedom of inquiry and interpretation should be unlimited, so long as man remains aware of his own limitations. The logical stability of this principle is not in disharmony with the whole purpose of God, including love and redemption of the individual, providing for an ever-growing fellowship, in fact, for one world. The process of personal development is dynamic, motivating individual initiative and encouraging social interaction. Therefore, a concern for the needs of the community weighs heavily upon the school and is at least one of the major reasons for its existence.

The foundation for Christian education is the unchanging aspect of the personality of God. Since God's nature and mind are perfect, we may assume lawful consistency. Inasmuch as no portion of his creation is completely known, but to some degree is knowable, everything calls for investigation tempered by humility. Although the subjective acts of prayer and worship, and the suprarational understanding of the richness of revelation, must never be completely formalized, they are not only germane to but must be central in Christian education. For through them is developed a mature loyalty to God as he is seen through the " mind of Christ." Here alone is to be found the larger unity long sought by the educator. The Christian fellowship avows those principles for education which can accept the problems of change and give a sense of direction. It can look at the whole person and at a complete universe. The modern community of believers sees in such a working knowledge an instrument for approaching the solutions to human problems and thus a way out of the frustrations of mankind. It provides for a means of the survival of man in the face of his present threats and gives him a sense of eternal destiny and a meaning to life's immediate concerns. Christian education therefore is worthy of man's best commitments.

To be sure, there are risks and hazards — for man is imperfect. One danger for all education lies in a possible narrow conceit, really in egocentricity which assumes too readily that truth has been grasped. Another peril is ever present — loss of contact with human emotion encountered in the daily round. Broad generalizations sometimes lose a grip upon life. People still have to make a living, renew professional skills, learn to get along with others on the job, choose marriage partners, rear children, learn the skills of appreciation of art and music, and know how to worship. Christianity not only can be but should be life-centered.

The community at large, within which the fellowship resides as a smaller segment, is a community of unrest. The constant fear of aggression from real or potential enemies holding divergent ideologies has driven groups to indoctrination in order to promote like-mindedness. The community at large is divided in its loyalties. The very loneliness of the one who is in the process of being educated, as well as his inability to accept change, tests the depth of meanings found in the institutions existing as a part of the body of Christ. Lack of deep abiding personal commitments springing from a central ideal has caused serious breakdown in modern society. The repercussions impinge upon the family, the church, and the school. Too many are satisfied with dwarfed ideals and care too little for their neighbors because their contacts with God are limited.

While it is recognized that our day places great value upon the individual, and while education is concerned with the intrinsic worth of the individual, Christian education assumes that personality never completely matures until egocentric patterns are merged with common devotions of the group dedicated to the best and most complete understanding of life. Education which calls itself Christian should actively confront the student with the nature of God as seen through Jesus Christ. Christian education can be education in its most enriching form. Perhaps a part of the resurgence of interest in religion, particularly for educators, has been induced by the study of the needs of man within his community and the knowledge of how he develops his larger loyalties, social and theocentric. Christian educational philosophy and procedure are indeed broad in scope. Exploration and application of underlying principles can fit well into the specific developmental processes as they are found on the elementary, secondary, and collegiate levels.

# CHRISTIAN PERSONALITY AND CHRISTIAN EDUCATION

## *Conrad Bergendoff*

PROBABLY at no point does the Christian student of today find himself more alien to modern culture than in his understanding of the nature of man. The Christian is amazed at the assumptions that underlie some of the methods employed in studying personality; for instance, it is assumed that by the behavior of animals we can understand the behavior of man. In this kind of thought by what criterion shall logic be judged? A contemporary psychologist admits that "addiction to machines, rats, or infants leads us to overplay those features of human behavior that are peripheral, signal-oriented, or genetic." [1] It is not my purpose to go into any detailed exposition of the purely anatomical interpretation of man. I emphasize only that it is the climate of our thought world. It is my position that the Christian idea of personality is worlds removed from such current theories of the nature of man.

The biological evolution of man is now taken for granted, and from it flows a whole philosophy of life that never questions how far its principle assumptions are tenable, and — more important — what conclusions are derived from them. [2] It may be the best hypothesis we can frame on which to assemble all the various facts of biology, and the Christian can look on all the assembled data with genuine interest, and hold for the moment the hypothesis that ties them together, without however being at all convinced that similarity of bones proves identity of destiny for all mammals.

### THE CHRISTIAN IDEA OF PERSONALITY

The Christian acknowledges the Scriptures as the source of his faith. The great fact in this reading of life is that man is an intelligent being created by an intelligent God. Man is not an isolated phenomenon in the universe. His creation belongs to a series that stretches back to a primeval nothingness. But as opposed to a philosophy which makes a god out of nothing, the Christian finds it more reasonable to believe that Being precedes creation, and that in the beginning God created heavens and earth and all that is therein. How and when this happened we cannot know, but Genesis speaks of a progression that leads from vegetable to animal to human life. Nor do we deny that man's body comes from the same earth; he who made the one also made the other, and there is a sense in which the dust that comes from the earth shall also return to it. But there is something unique in the story of Creation which is material to the uniqueness of man all through the centuries. Man is not only clay. He is not only one of the forms of animals. He is created with qualities not possessed by any other created thing. He is given dominance over the animal world, and the power of distinguishing between the objects that are created and the task of naming them. Above all he is endowed with an ability to know something of the nature and the will of the Power which creates and sustains and orders the universe. The Biblical language expresses this nature as " the image of God." Man is not himself God, for an image is different from that which it resembles. But the image of God in man makes him sensitive to communication from God and responsible to the will of God. This is the glory of man, that which characterizes him and makes him *man*. No description of man that ignores his unparalleled relationship both to creation and to the Creator can be called Christian, and no philosophy of Christian education is true to its name that does not start from this faith.

The Christian conception of man finds itself at odds with that secularistic philosophy which assumes man to be solely mechanistic and his behavior measurable only in terms of stimulus and reaction. Or that he is a bundle of inherited impulses seeking expression in the urge to eat, to reproduce, to kill, or to die. Or that all the varied, fascinating play of human activity is but as the lambent, colored flames that arise as human energy consumes itself, transforming physical force into the sexual, social, artistic forms of the moment. On these assumptions the ancient humors — choleric, phlegmatic, sanguine, melancholic — may, indeed, be channeled into new categories of glandular activity, body size, sensory preferences, while statistical studies may seek every manner of correlation between physical traits and behavior. Yet the results cannot explain the true nature of man, his aspirations, and the higher purposes of his actions. Especially in what is termed the abnormal, man is supposed to reveal himself, and to a layman it sometimes seems that the normal study of man is the study of the abnormal. But "normal" is itself an ambiguous term. If in psychology we repudiate all norms or laws except the statistical, and find by comparing that men divide themselves into various degrees of differences, what does normal mean but a sort of statistical average of the moment? Some psychologists despair even of mathematical statements and resort to a kind of picture language where the direction of an individual is indicated as he responds to his environment. Underlying all this proceeding is a common endeavor to compare men with each other, relate them to one another, and to describe human personality in terms of similarity or dissimilarity of response to surrounding pressures.[3]

## The Validity of Standards

The fundamental distinction between every non-Christian psychology and Christian psychology concerns the matter of standards. We can learn much from studies in personality by those who make no reference to Christianity, and all observations on human traits or instincts or types are of interest to the Christian educator. But there is in the Christian outlook something unexampled, incomparable, even absolute, which differentiates it from any secular point of view. Our whole definition of Christian personality hinges on this primordial element.

For Christianity is the religion of the revelation of a Person who is the standard of measurement of man. Man is not known by comparing one individual with another, or one group with another with the view to arriving at some kind of average. We know man, as Christians, by the Son of Man, who is the Judge of all mankind. This is the essential meaning of the incarnation. Here is the norm by which we know what man is meant to be and for what purpose he is created. The central truth of Christianity is Christ, apart from whom there is no Christian truth. The figure of Christ is the image that determines man's image of himself. *Ecce homo,* "Behold the man," is more than Pilate's half-scornful, half-pitying identification of a rejected teacher. It is the confession of what constitutes manhood. In the parable of the Last Judgment all are judged by their conscious or unconscious relationship to him. There is a universal norm by which man is measured.

A generation that understands little of dogmatics ridicules the theological controversies of Nicaea, wondering how men could ever become so excited about an iota. Was Christ *homoousios* or *homoiousios?* of the same substance as God or like God? Yet in that controversy lay a very significant difference between an absolute and a relative conception of not only the nature of Christ's personality, but also of the nature of man's. For if Christ were only a reflection of the divine Person there was no essential difference between him and every created person. He might be a better individual, a more admirable character, but yet one with us. What Athanasius contended for, and what the Christian Church has taught ever since, is that Christ is Judge over us and hence has an authority we do not possess. We are not with him fellow prisoners at the bar of some unknown court of nature and history, liable to all the vagaries of chance, or victims of transient lords or of some unknowable process. We are at his court, before the bar of his decree, of like nature with him so as to understand ourselves by him, but subject to him as Lord of our being and Judge of our destiny.

A seventeenth century hymn writer, Joachim Neander, said:

> "Lord, great wonders workest Thou!
> To Thy sway all creatures bow;
> Write Thou deeply in my heart
> What I am, and what Thou art."

What man is, and also what God's nature is, is revealed to us in Jesus Christ. He reveals the heart and mind of the Unsearchable One — he reveals our relationship to himself. The Letter to the Hebrews distinguishes clearly between Christ's nature and man's — " He who sanctifies and those who are sanctified have all one origin." Yet, it continues, " That is why he is not ashamed to call them brethren." He " partook of the same nature " as theirs in order that he might " deliver all those who through fear of death were subject to lifelong bondage " (ch. 2). His identification with man through the incarnation establishes a relationship with men in which he can communicate with them. But he is more than any of them — else he had no more authority than any of them. He is in an incomparable way the Word of God, " living and active, sharper than any two-edged sword, piercing to the division of soul and spirit, of joints and marrow, and discerning the thoughts and intentions of the heart. And before him no creature is hidden, but all are open and laid bare to the eyes of him with whom we have to do " (Heb. 4:12, 13).

For the Christian this thought of Christ is Alpha and Omega, the beginning of personal existence and the eschatological judgment which also is present in each moment. To borrow the language of psychology, life outside of Christ is abnormal, while life in the consciousness of an unbroken relationship to him is the norm for man's life. The New Testament does not hesitate to call this a new birth — so radical is the break between a Christless and a Christian experience. Christ becomes the core around which a life is organized, the integrating power that relates everything to his authority, making the thoughts of the mind and desires of the heart subject to himself. Here is the objective reality outside man which psychology vainly gropes to apprehend but cannot, as long as it refuses to posit any reality beyond man's own existence. Luther with profound insight describes the hopeless condition of man as being due to his *incurvatus in se* — man's turning in upon himself. If that is man's only devise, he becomes more and more involved and entangled within himself, and finally sinks into the slough of despond. But in Christianity there does appear One outside ourselves, whose outreached hand saves us from our own weight.

Christian higher education needs today a clearer declaration of its relationship to Christ. We are too timid, as Christian educators, in affirming the Personality of Christ as the foundation of Christian learning. Somehow the prestige and pretensions of a learning which assumes to be judge of Christ have made us speechless. The culture of Rome and Greece, of Renaissance and Rationalism, is supposed to be superior to the truth of the gospel, and we are delighted when the wise men of the ages condescend to say a favorable word for the Christian teaching. I am not pleading for anything but humility in learning; the pride of Christians is usually learned from manners not Christian. But Christian higher education today needs ask no favor of those who know not Christ, and the concept of truth need not be borrowed from such as are ignorant of the true God and true man.

## Christian History and Personality

Especially in the field of personality will the Christian find that little advance has been made beyond what Christian history has afforded. Modern descriptions of the disintegration of personality assume an idea of personality which is the result of Christian anthropology. I almost venture the assertion that only in a Christian culture, or a culture deeply influenced by Christianity, is there a study of personality. I believe a case could be made for the assertion that our ideas of personality are a result of the Christian doctrine of the Person of Christ. It was his appearance that made men conscious of the meaning of their own thoughts.

We are sometimes told that the modern notion of personality derives from the Renaissance. Then men began to see with new eyes — the world of nature, the composition of their own bodies, the relationship of the individual to the mass out of which he emerged. We are told, too, that it was a rebirth of interest in classical paganism that helped to liberate modern man from medieval scholasticism. But it is significant that the Renaissance grew in Christian soil. The Renaissance personality, for all its dependence on Greek and Roman sources, was something else than Greece or Rome knew. It may be impossible — and unnecessary — to untangle Christian and pagan motifs in the Renaissance geniuses, but a leaven of the gospel had been at work for centuries before the modern European became aware of himself. Granted even that much of Renaissance humanism was atheistic, you cannot be an atheist before you have been a theist. When in the fifteenth century men thought themselves " gods," even their conception of their own divine powers was a result of a divine revelation in Jesus Christ. Even today men like to think of their own divine nature and take to themselves qualities first apparent in an integrated personality in Jesus Christ. Despite all the worldliness they may reflect, modern doctrines of man nevertheless must confess, " And from his fullness have we all received, grace upon grace " (John 1:16).

## THE REVELATION OF PERSONALITY IN CHRIST

Back of all our faith in the possibility of a personality — an integrated whole with some discernible pattern of meaning — stands a figure who was a whole, and made others whole. Whitehead tells us that modern science of the universe is founded on a theological notion of order in the universe.[4] Is it not equally true that the modern science of man rests ultimately on the belief that in the flux of force there is an integrating principle that makes the self one? The Christian self is in Christ a new creation. Christ is God's communication to man of what man is meant to reflect. If today we have vague ideas of humanity, it is because we see the Christ so dimly. The gospel record has become a palimpsest, overwritten by so much of modern speculation that it needs to be restored in its original purity and power if it is to have the power to create wherever it is allowed to give forth its true splendor and radiance. " There is only one image," says V. V. Zenkovsky, " which is both ' beautiful ' and a constant source of nourishment for the moral sphere, and that is the image of Christ the Saviour. In relation to this image we can accept the indivisibility of the aesthetic and moral spheres — but only in relation to him! Only the image of the Saviour, his inexpressible beauty and his immeasurable love and service to mankind, can inspire us with an equal devotion." [5]

In the West, Kierkegaard bears eloquent testimony to the same conviction, that much of what is called religion in European culture is an aestheticism that is divorced from Christ, the only " Beautiful One." Or may we say that we have an idea of beauty that is neither moral nor religious? In Christianity the beauty of holiness is in an image which " had no form or comeliness that we should look at him, and no beauty that we should desire him " (Isa. 53:2). Yet this same image " reflects the glory of God and bears the very stamp of his nature " (Heb. 1:3), which may lead us to wonder if we do not judge God by our ideas of glory rather than let him determine what is truly the glorious nature " upholding the universe."

The Christian personality is created around the image of Christ. This is the nucleus, or core, around which gradually all the experiences of life are to be organized. " In the image of God he created him," we read in Gen. 1:27, and the Christian personality is God's creation in the image of Jesus Christ. Arnold Toynbee quotes in his *Study of History* a friend's comment: " There seem to be two kinds of mystic: one of them attains the annihilation of personality, the other the fulfillment of personality in the Vision of God." [6] I accept as my definition of the Christian personality: the individual who attains the fulfillment of his own self in the revelation of God in Jesus Christ.

The Christian faith saves us from making religion merely a mystic gazing at even the image of the glory of God; it does so by the doctrine of the Holy Spirit. That vision stirs movements which the Christian cannot explain. " Behold, the Lamb of God " is an injunction which immediately has something to do with the words that follow: " who takes away the sin of the world! " (John 1:29). The Holy Spirit is a creative power outside ourselves, which creates a new life. Or, properly understood, it is a life of new forms and colors, for the forms are the actions that the Spirit inspires in those whose faces are fixed on Christ and the colors are the new feelings that his love moves in our breasts. For the Christian life is a new creation, the kind fervently prayed for in the hymns addressed " Veni, Creator Spiritus." We have only dimly perceived the power and riches and glory of human life as it can be where man lives in communion with the Creator Spirit. His work was not finished in one day or one week, but his is that inexhaustible power welling forth in all human endeavor which can, where acknowledged as God, reshape both mind and body. This faith is wholly other than a reading of man's actions as the involuntary movement of waves driven by subconscious forces. Nor is it a yielding to chance stimuli which always produce similar automatic responses. It is a faith that recognizes a conflict within man of forces greater than himself, but a faith that reveals to man a power that can save him both from himself and powers outside. Indeed, only in terms of this kind of conflict can we talk about personality. For personality implies a turning from, and a turning to, and it is in the crucial and repeated moments of turning that character is formed. The most profound theology— of masters of thought such as Augustine, Luther, Calvin, and Pascal — hesitates to call this procedure freedom of choice, for man hardly shows the ability of choice. But there are set before man two ways, two goals, two masters. Human drama deals with man's decision, conscious or unconscious. Human tragedy marks that decision, and there personality is born and nourished. Outside that context the term has little meaning.[7]

## CONCEPTIONS OF GOOD AND EVIL

Christian thought is necessarily dualistic. When it has penetrated to the farthest frontiers of human experience it still finds a conflict between good and evil. From the very beginning to the very end of humanity's existence we find the presence of a force contrary to the will of God and consequently hostile to the welfare of man. But the nature of this conflict has often been misinterpreted. It has been portrayed, both outside Christian thought and within, as a conflict between man's physical nature and a metaphysical one, often called spiritual. It has been described as the struggle between an invisible something called soul and the visible material structure of the body. The physical has been identified as the evil; the " spiritual," as the good. Christian psychology has suffered immeasurably by this kind of thinking, and the history of Christianity is full of the stories of asceticism by which individuals or groups have sought to mortify the body in the name of a holy life.

The story is too long and complicated to be reviewed here.[8] But

I stress its importance for a study of Christian psychology. It is my own conviction that the Bible gives no ground to support this kind of dualism, which places the conflict between body and spirit. The Biblical antithesis is between spirit and flesh, which is the same as between good and evil. Evil is no more synonymous with the body (nor is flesh the same as body) than good is one with spirit. The innermost conflict between good and evil is in spirit as well as in body, though mind or spirit cannot, in human thought, be divorced from body. All human thought is bodily thought, for man thinks through organs of the body. But there is in man, considered as a totality, as a unity, a struggle between authorities to be obeyed, goals to be achieved. Every part of the body is involved, for the decision affects body as well as mind.

Christianity has much to oppose in modern materialism. But it can also learn from materialism that man is a unity of body and mind. When Christian thought disassociates mind from the body, it becomes unreal and so ethereal as to be fruitless. The incarnation of Christ should have cautioned Christian thinkers not to let Neoplatonic ideas determine the ideal of the Christian life as a state out of the body. The Christian believes that God created the body, that Christ came in a body, that there will be a resurrection of the body. Redemption must be defined in bodily terms. There is need of a Christian psychology that will bring the doctrine of man down from the clouds of spiritualism and lodge it in the appetites, the needs, the desires, the decisions, the actions, the sufferings, of man. Some idealistic Christianity has lifted man off the ground and thereby lost its power. Christian personality finds its ground and its field of action here in the everyday world where the Master lived. Man and nature are not in themselves evil — the miracle of redemption is the winning of man and the use of nature to the will of God.

Interestingly, it is not only Christian theology that has tended to loosen the bonds between body and spirit. While much of modern thought has become increasingly materialistic and mechanistic, modern art has taken refuge in abstractions as little related to concrete life as some "spiritual" theology. The result has a bearing on the conception of personality. Maurice Stern, writing on Cézanne, won-

ders at the disappearance of " the complex psyche of man " from
the visual arts. In modern art, he claims, " the important fact that
truly great painters did not have to dematerialize the body in order
to enhance the soul was overlooked. Giotto, Masaccio, and Michel-
angelo did not have to sacrifice the body as a burnt offering to the
spirit. They revealed that the spirit can and does dwell within the
body of man, that the one enhances the other, that the two are in-
separable while we are still alive. . . . The old masters reveal far
deeper penetration of character." [9]

## The Unity of Body and Mind

Ever since Descartes's philosophy split man's nature in two, theology has followed suit. Philosophy has wanted to become a science
of the mind, theology a science of the soul. Science has been left
with matter and psychology with the body. From a Christian point
of view this is an inadmissible distinction and the result is intoler-
able. What the Creator has joined together man may not separate.
Christian thinkers have no greater mission today than to study man
as a unity of body and mind, and science must be cured of its blind-
ness in dealing with man as soulless. Delacroix is reported once to
have said that " every human face with a few simple changes could
be made to resemble the face of an animal." [10] Those few simple
changes have been made in much of modern biology and psychology.
Christian scholarship must restore the image of man to humanity.

The Bible gives much space, not to the origin of man, but to his
goal. His destiny is of more consequence than his past, though none
will deny the importance of the past. A great gulf divides Christian
thought from current biological doctrines, which conceal a fatalism
inherent in the thought that man is the creature of derived impulses spending themselves in his life. One of the by-products of
evolutionism is an uncritical notion that man comes into his natural
or social world and is driven by instincts, almost like a car running
amuck. Causes of various kinds impel him on to an inexorable fate.
Such is not the Christian belief. The will of God seeks man out, ap-
peals to him, attracts him to a life wherein all his gifts and powers
can be employed for his own development. The Son of Man is

described as one who attracts all men to himself, as a magnet draw-ing the individual to a heavenly Kingdom. Paganism is fatalistic, whether it be Greek or American. Christianity is a faith that is teleological; the end, rather than the beginning, shapes the course of human life. The Christian personality is oriented toward Christ. "Forgetting what lies behind and straining to what lies ahead, I press on toward the goal for the prize of the upward call of God in Christ Jesus," is Paul's classic definition of Christian experience. "Not that . . . I am already perfect; but I press on . . . because Christ Jesus has made me his own" (Phil. 3:12–14). The pull of an eternal love is the motive power, as opposed to the push of a primor-dial urge. To be possessed by Christ is something far different from being possessed by dark powers of a subhuman realm. The existence of such powers is not denied. Paul expressly refers to such, and realizes that the Christian must contend "against the world rulers of this present darkness, against the spiritual hosts of wicked-ness in the heavenly places" (Eph. 6:12). But it is resistance to these forces that marks Christian personality. Submission to them destroys any kind of personality.

## The Marks of Christian Personality

It is in this context that we need to restudy the Christian doctrines of original sin and the forgiveness of sins as they bear on the develop-ment of personality. For "original sin" is not a scientific term ap-plied to man as a biological creature. It is a religious term applied by a Christian to himself as he thinks of his utter inability to over-come the forces that prevent him from doing the will of God. It is no mystical quality of human physical nature that has to be physically expunged from man. It is the tendency of man to follow the apparent present good as against the eternal God, the inclination to idolatry in its infinite number of forms. It is not the real nature of man, not the nature God intends. Hence man is pulled by both forces, until he may cry, "Who shall deliver me from this fearful conflict?" But the power of Christ is strong. It can turn the will of man toward his own. And pursuing the direction of Him who called us with a holy calling, we find unceasing forgiveness for our stumblings, our falling, our sins. The life of the Christian is a repetition of forgiveness — and of being raised again. The direction is what matters, though the goal be distant. Daily renewal, constant intention, unending hope, these, much more than blameless actions and unearthly holiness, are the marks of Christian personality. A pilgrim following a vision is our best simile as we try to picture the nature of the Christian.

This is the background of anything that we may say about the significance of personality in the learning process. For only thus does it become clear that the difference between the Christian and the non-Christian student is not in the heavens or earth or sea, or in anything in the universe that may be the object of study, but in personal orientation. There are no fields of thought closed to the Christian; indeed, he more than any other feels free to investigate everywhere. But he sees with different eyes, for it is in the light of Christ that he beholds the created world and human history. He knows himself in that light. How can a man know anything except in relationship to himself? What a man thinks in his heart about himself affects all other knowledge he may learn. The Christian is a free man, delivered from the bondage of the fear of death (Heb. 2:15), and in the affirmation of life he sees all things in the light of the Giver of life. Here is the true freedom of the liberal arts, the Truth that makes men free.

Here again we need to emphasize the indivisibility of the Christian person. For the freedom he enjoys is to be developed in his bodily state. Education may be thought of as the liberating of his powers and the employment of them in the creation of a rich life. It is through long and arduous training of mind and muscle that the musician learns to express himself skillfully and richly. Just so, the Christian learns to use all his senses, muscles, and nerves to exercise completely his powers in discovering the possibilities of human achievement. Each experience relates itself to the main purpose of his life. Personality develops in the degree that all the thoughts and emotions find a unity in this relationship to a divine Person and Companion. From this nucleus comes the energy expressing itself in attitudes and acts toward others. A consistent pattern slowly emerges; a character is formed that marks the Christian. Mistakes there may be, and at times failure more evident than triumph. But in the heart of faith is a new creation, and a new earth come slowly to view. Here is a positive answer to the negativist spirit of an age that sees a great nothingness as the end of man's life, in which personality at best is but a heroic gesture defying fate, but succumbing to extinction when the vital force is gone. The Christian personality is based on a faith in life, and organized around a relationship to Him who once created life and again asserted himself above death. The difference between human personalities is essentially the difference between human despair — the conquest of man by fate — and human faith, the conquest of nature by the will of God.

# 6

# THE LEARNER–TEACHER RELATIONSHIP

## *William E. Hulme*

M AN, who is created in the image of God, is also created as an individual. Individuality, however, is something into which we are continually growing in an environment of personal relationships. When they are positive in nature, such relationships are for us the source of confidence and incentives necessary for our development. We require the assurance of belonging to others to be secure within, and we need security within to be free to grow in individuality. What, then, is the problem of the learner-teacher relationship?

For the Christian educator it has, certainly, dimensions beyond those we classify as psychosocial. In the first place, a Christian structure admits the role of religion, which ties in immediate with ultimates and alone promises coherence in all areas. In the second place, Christian commitment if genuine turns to account that creative activity of the Holy Spirit which is an ongoing, never-ending process within the teacher and the learner and has potentials not confined to the classroom.

### A CREATIVE RELATIONSHIP

All personal relationships that have any influence in our lives are in varying degrees learner-teacher relationships, be they those of parent and child, husband and wife, friend and friend, or professor and student: each member of such bonds receives something from the other that is educative. The reciprocal nature of the learning factor may not always be immediately and impressively obvious; however, it is bound sooner or later to become evident even in the teacher forced to admit, at least to himself, that he has learned something from his students. With such an awareness a creative relationship may begin and continue as a means for the development of personality.

The conception of creative human relatedness in the educative process precludes any disposition to regard education simply as the transmission of knowledge from one person to another. To be sure, we no longer regard the mind of the student as a *tabula rasa* to be filled in by the teacher. We know that that mind is already occupied, that it is the mind of a person with a history, the nature of which has much to do with how and what he learns. That person enters the classroom with emotional patterns already developed, with both conscious and unconscious needs, and with goals both immediate and long-range, all of which have a selective influence in the activity of learning. Whether or not the pupil learns depends upon whether or not he is receptive to the learning, and this receptivity in turn depends upon whether or not the substance of his learning fits into the dynamics of his personality.

Although the student may have been inhibited in his individuality, he undoubtedly retains some capacity for knowing what he needs. Whether he is able to articulate his needs or not, his interests and concerns will center around them, and whenever he perceives an affinity for them in the knowledge that is presented, he will learn. This is the well-known psychology of the enthusiasm for learning, which is the most important factor in the process next to natural endowment in intelligence. But we may not always know the hidden factors that arrest it.

Take Bob, for example. He had trouble fitting into life at college. He could concentrate on his academic pursuits or on his social development, but he could not seem to harmonize the two. If he tried to force himself to study, he developed severe anxiety. Instead of concentrating he would berate himself for neglecting his social development. The counseling process revealed that work and social life had been pitted against each other in Bob's home. In the college setting Bob's conflict over work and social development became the conflict over study and social development. When he was helped to see how his college assignments fitted into his own needs and goals, he gained a whole new outlook upon his academic venture and was able to channel his efforts and his social experience into one creative process.

The Christian teacher who is by commitment in creative relationship to the learner, and thus aware of the role of the Holy Spirit in the relationship, will also realize his limitations — that he is a contributor to the process but not the director of it. Moreover, he will rely on resources beyond his limitations. For this reason he will not be so susceptible to discouragement as those whose reliance is limited to their own role. He neither presumes to be the Holy Spirit nor to judge him. When the teacher so views the student, he sees him as a child of God and treats him with increased respect for his individuality. Rather than identify him in terms of how he compares with some arbitrary standards of evaluation, he will receive him as one who is beyond comparison. Each student is a story in himself. Since we are often able to sense where we stand in another's estimation, a wholesome personal respect inspires confidence. As the learning process is bigger than the particular subject we teach, so the person of the student is a larger issue than the knowledge we are attempting to give him. In fact, an essential in all learning is the awareness of the limitations of our learning. The unification of knowledge in religion, buttressed by the creative relationship of learner-teacher, preserves both learner and teacher from the distortions of disconnected learning and the pretensions of fragmentary living.

## A Defensive Relationship

Both learner and teacher approach their relationship together, each knowing that he will create an impression in the other's mind. Since both are seeking goals which they feel are contingent upon this circumstance, they naturally want it to be favorable. Both have some preconceived notions concerning their chances for making a favorable start. Most of us have at times some misgivings over our own value and approach the relationship with at least something of apprehension. In addition to his concern over how he will impress the teacher, the student may also be fearful about the impression he will create in the minds of his classmates. If his past experience with such relationships has left him feeling inadequate, he may have a defensive attitude and be inclined to interpret situations negatively. There is the teacher, for example, who becomes touchy when asked a question about grading in a test, when all that is involved is a point of information. There is also the student who interprets the teacher's correction as a personal affront.

A student who actually failed in a course explained that it was because of an embarrassing incident early in the term, which convinced him that both the teacher and the class regarded him as stupid. On one occasion he had informed the teacher before the class period that he was not prepared. The teacher apparently forgot about him and in class proceeded to quiz and embarrass him. Humiliated and angered, he lost his incentive for the course. When the teacher noticed his indifference, he tried to draw him out with more questions, succeeding only in persuading him of his own inferiority and the teacher's determination to expose it. Convinced that he had no chance, he dreaded the class and believed himself unable to do any constructive work.

When a teacher tries to move his pupil to learn by berating him for his poor response, he probably will only retard him more. When, on the other hand, he uses an obviously supportive approach, he may raise feelings of inadequacy in the learner. As an example, there is the student whose mother had great ambitions for him. When he did not fulfill her expectations, she blamed the teachers or belittled other children. The child resented the notion that he needed such support and began to hate both himself and his mother — himself for being unable to meet her expectations, and his mother for undermining his confidence through her patronizing attitude. In the classroom he gave every impression that he needed support and then reacted negatively to every teacher who offered any. Having no tangible justification for his resentment, he felt guilty and deflated.

Since it is concern for our own self-respect that makes us defensive when we approach the learner-teacher relationship, we may rush into precautions which to others seem self-defeating. A case in point is the all-too-common gifted student content with a caliber of work obviously beneath his capabilities. Often he is in doubt about his own capability. So long as he applies himself only enough to pass, he can always comfort himself in the thought that he could do better if he really tried. Since he enjoys the reputation of having superior ability without having the grades, he has nothing to gain and everything to lose in putting his ability to the test. In the same category is the teacher who readily admits that he could do a better job if he had a lighter load and smaller classes. At the same time he resists any attempt to lighten his load or his course enrollments, for he too does not want to step out from behind his ego-protecting excuse and expose himself to a threatening situation.

The severest blow of all to a student's ego is evidence of his dullness in the presence of his teachers and fellow students, and his greatest loss is the loss of respect in his academic community. Even when one appears to be rude or conceited, he may simply be compensating for his own uncertainty over his ability. When afraid to stand on his ability alone, the lagger may resort to other means, to what has come to be known as apple-polishing or any of the many forms of attempted ingratiation which lower the respect of the students and teachers alike. Since the fear of inadequacy takes many disguises, the teacher may err in evaluating its symptoms apart from their causes. To illustrate: Because of early emotional disturbances Joan found school too much for her to cope with. As a result she adopted the familiar escape of daydreaming, and was promptly prodded to stop it. The outcome was that she learned to simulate interest and attention, and in time turned into so excellent an actress that when she entered college no one would have suspected she was miles away in her spirit and fathoms deep in fear of discovery.

The element of the defensive can scarcely be avoided. When a teacher gives a poor grade, the student is going to feel bad. There is no way he can be spared from such a reality, and there is probably no way to prevent the recipient's momentary resentment toward the teacher and the course. What he needs is neither rebuke nor reassurance, but rather empathic understanding. "I know you feel bad about this grade, and I understand," will do far more to heal the wound than any attempt to minimize it. We are teaching principles of life. No one can vindicate giving a low mark as a retaliation, nor can he defend withholding a poor grade because of the suffering it will cause. Giving a grade is a matter of allowing the student to reap what he has sowed in terms of what the teacher feels is an intellectual appropriation of the knowledge of the course. Let the teacher grade without apology. If he omits this lesson in life, his students will be even less able to accept disappointment when they are confronted with it later. In addition, students do not like teachers who give them more than they deserve. And they know.

When an inquirer asks for a justification of his grading, he needs to be handled with patience. What he really wants to see us about is an ego wound. We are dealing with an emotional problem. He needs the opportunity to express his bewilderment or resentment and to receive as objectively as possible our reasons for our appraisal of his work. Often he is more interested in discovering whether the teacher still respects him or not than he is in any answer to his question.

### A Teacher-initiated Relationship

The quality of the relationship between a learner and a teacher depends normally on what is initiated by the teacher. The learner's attitude toward the relationship is usually conditioned by what he has felt the teacher's attitude toward him to be. Yet each instructor is not necessarily responsible for the caliber of the relationship that exists, since the learner's impression may have been formed by earlier learner-teacher situations and may cause the learner to approach subsequent ones with a preconceived attitude. A teacher-initiated relationship can be a medium for and a pattern of the creative work of the Holy Spirit: God initiates and the individual responds. He offers us his love without reservations. When we receive it, we love him in return. Grace animates the faith that receives it. Actually it is God's faith in us that inspires our faith in him. " We love him, because he first loved us " (I John 4:19). The result is the receiver's desire to receive more from the Giver. " Show me thy ways, O Lord; teach me thy paths " (Ps. 25:4).

Most teachers have probably had the gratifying experience of noting marked improvement in students who have been reassured of their instructor's personal interest. *Reader's Digest* (Public Affairs Pamphlet No. 211) reports a survey made of two hundred boys in a slum area. According to usual expectations, ninety per cent of them would spend time in the penitentiary. After twenty-five years one hundred and eighty of the number were investigated again. Only four had ever been in jail. Seventy-five per cent of the men gave credit for their good conduct to the same teacher. After she was located and asked why she thought the men still remembered her, she could not account for it. Yet, as she reflected upon the days that were gone, she said, " I loved those boys."   *7 8 7 5 0*

Our Lord had a way of opening the hearts of those whom he taught. Before he gave his discourse in the upper room on the night of his betrayal, he washed the feet of his disciples. The learner-teacher relationship is a learner-leader relationship. At times it may even be that of the disciple leading the master. Normally the leader is the master who initiates the relationship and who, in having something to give, attracts the receivers. But he is also the learner and must have in order to give. The cultivation of his own growth is indispensable to the learning potential in his relationship to his students. If he relies on substitutes for this growth — friendliness, affability, or fluency in superficial speech — he will ultimately impoverish his work. When Jesus put his relationship to his disciples to the test, only what he had to give held the Twelve. After the feeding of the five thousand he made his followers choose between the political and spiritual understanding of his Messiahship. After this many forsook him. Turning to his intimate circle, he said, " Will ye also go away? " Peter answered, " Lord, to whom shall we go? thou hast the words of eternal life " (John 6:67, 68). Jesus even forsook his sleep to prepare himself to give to those he was leading. The Gospels record more than once how he either spent the night in prayer or went out a great while before day to renew his spirit (Mark 1:35; 6:46; Luke 5:16; 6:12). Out of these experiences of communion he was able to give, and his disciples were inspired to receive.

The teacher's growth, however, is not only in the area of his own subject, important as this is, but also in his religious role in the educative process. The quality of the learner-teacher relationship depends on the teacher's continuous search in both areas. He who can initiate a productive relationship with his learner is one who loves his subject and cares that his followers learn it. His enthusiasm is contagious. The fact that he cares that his students learn the subject moves them also to care. As Emerson said, it is the spirit that teaches.

When our concern is motivated by love, there is no ego image to live up to. When a student does not respond, we think first of his welfare and not of our own. We will not assume the blame for what he has not yet learned, unless we know of some definite way in which we have failed to make the material clear. Even then the learning process is a double responsibility. No teacher, not even Jesus himself, could assume the responsibility for the outcome of all his learner-teacher relationships. To do so is egocentric, for it places on the teacher's shoulders what the Creator never intended to be there. Otherwise each could not give account for himself.

## A Mutual Respect Relationship

When the motive of the teacher is love, he respects the personality of his pupil, even as he exploits it when he is motivated by his ego. The student manifesting extreme negative or positive characteristics in the evaluating scale is the one most likely to capture his interest. As a result the teacher may not give equal attention to all his charges; indeed, he may be led to unfair discrimination. A corrective for the teacher lies in his respect for the total personality of the student, including personal responsibility. Nothing we give to the learner can replace his own integrative activity, and, being a part of the growth process, integration is often painful. Consequently the learner may shy away from responsibility, and the teacher may desire to spare him the ordeal. But learning the hard way may be the only way one can learn. The growing pains that come through exercising our own responsibilities are the fear and trembling with which we work out our own salvation. The Creator's purpose to save us by grace in no way violates our individual responsibility, for this grace is received only through the personal decision of faith.

A situation of mutual respect will encourage self-expression which can lead to insights of reality that we may not otherwise achieve. But if the student is to speak with ease in the teacher's presence, the teacher must acquire the habit of listening, which is difficult for one who normally thinks of himself as the speaker and of his students as listeners. Thus, when he gives a listener an opportunity to express himself, the eager preceptor may chafe at the bit, hardly able to wait until he can get back into the speaking role. Apparently he believes he has things to say that are more important than what the student is saying. Perhaps he has. On the other hand, he may be interrupting the process of learning. If in impatience he anticipates wrongly what the student has in mind, he may precipitate a further blockage. Actually the teacher is bound to learn from his pupils' self-expression, for when they combine his thought with their own reflective thinking, they turn it into a new product through the process of expression.

This mutual exchange of learning, the outcome of a mutual respect, is usually teacher-initiated. When our students discover that they can teach us a few things, and particularly when we acknowledge their contribution, it is to them a tremendous lift in confidence and a renewed incentive to learning. However, such an end is only possible when there is respect for the teacher and his knowledge.

If learning is an individual experience that is incomplete without self-expression, then smaller classes or seminars would appear to offer more opportunity for the development of the learner-teacher relationships than large classes, but only when and if teachers, students, and administrators take the small class as seriously as the large class. There is always the danger of exploiting the friendly atmosphere of the seminar and the small group by relying on it rather than on thorough preparation. However, smaller classes of fifteen to twenty-five students lend themselves more to the atmosphere of acceptance than larger classes of thirty to forty-five students. Whatever facilitates the teacher's cultivation of mutual respect fosters the security and self-expression that lead to growth. It is within the relationship of mutual respect that blocks to growth are removed and the creative process is set in motion.

## CONCLUSION

The knowledge transmitted in the learner-teacher relationship is incorporated by the learner into the creative process at work within him. His receptivity is in proportion to his recognition of how the knowledge at hand fits into his needs, interests, and goals. The teacher with a Christian commitment is in a position to relate his subject to the universal quest for ultimate values and ideals. His relationship with his students is an aspect of the working of God's Spirit in meeting the needs of man. The defensiveness with which teacher and learner approach their relationship can hinder the educative experience. Feelings of inadequacy may prevent both from exposing themselves to the hazards of all-out effort. Subtle external coercion usually fails to release the student from his blockage and may intensify it.

The learner-teacher relationship that is a stimulant to growth is patterned after the redemptive relationship of God to man. God gives, and man receives, and in receiving he responds. As the leader in this relationship, the teacher faces the responsibility of fostering his own growth so that he may contribute to the growth of the learner. He demonstrates his love in his respect for his students and in his concern for their learning. Self-expression encouraged by respect leads to insights into knowledge. Thus the learner-teacher relationship contributes both to the growth of knowledge and to the maturing of individuality.

# PART
# III

# *Method*

# 7

## CURRICULUM IN THE CHRISTIAN COLLEGE

### *Merrimon Cuninggim*

THE problems of curriculum in the Christian college are one
problem, namely, how to give tangible expression to the Christian philosophy of education which the college has consciously
adopted. For to be a Christian college is to have adopted a Christian
philosophy of education. No other definition of a Christian college
makes any sense. A college is not Christian merely by virtue of its
organic tie with some denomination, nor does it fail to be so merely
by absence of such a bond. This is not to say that the possession of an
official relationship with some Church body is irrelevant or useless.
On the contrary, a Church-related college is more likely, by that
very token, to be sensitive to Christian principles of education and
to the Christian faith in general. The sponsoring denomination
should serve as a source of continual reminder to the institution, lest
or when it should forget its Christian character. But its character,
not its sponsorship, is the decisive factor. Elemental to any discussion of the Christian college, therefore, is the Christian philosophy
of education which informs and motivates it.

Thus when in the present study we come to an examination of the
curriculum, it is within the scope of a prior consideration of fundamental educational philosophy. The curriculum is simply the instrument through which the purpose of the institution is made manifest
to its students. If in truth this purpose is Christian, then the curriculum will give evidence of it. Thus it is that the problems of the
curriculum can be said to constitute one overarching problem: How
can the curriculum be made to embody and further the Christian
philosophy of the college?

## WHAT IS A CHRISTIAN COLLEGE?

It is tempting to rush headlong into a discussion of this central question. It is inviting to limit one's remarks to a single premise — The Christian college must be Christian — and to explore the meaning which this premise alone possesses for the curriculum. But though such is obviously my major task, another premise calls for at least passing comment. For there are two presuppositions, not just one, which the words " Christian college " properly call to mind. The other is the proposition: The Christian college must be a college. Nothing in a Christian philosophy of education should, or need, contravene what is legitimately meant by education. A Christian college is no less a college by virtue of its seeking to be Christian.

Why take the time even to say such a thing? There are those who possess doubts at this point. They suspect that when we talk about making a college Christian, we mean somehow to manipulate truth to suit ourselves and our Christian prejudices, and to shut off the free search for truth when it begins to get embarrassing. Let it be stated categorically: A Christian college must be as loyal to facts and in the shaping of its curriculum as devoted to the pursuit of knowledge, wherever it may lead, as any other kind of institution — and even more so than any other. When education becomes Christian, it does not change to superstition, or indoctrination, or whimsical piety. It remains what it is in essence; it simply becomes better education. The Christian college must be a college, and the very best kind of college. Now loyalty to the facts and the free search for truth are the marks of all education; they are not the property merely of Christian education, and, further, their presence in a college situation is not *ipso facto* justification for that institution's claiming to be Christian. Once upon a time some of our secular universities were wont to defend themselves against charges of godlessness by pointing out that they taught respect for the truth, and surely that was a very Christian thing. Even now one occasionally hears some college official claim that his curriculum serves the cause of Christianity merely because it is honestly informative. But this is garbled thinking. To love the true and hate the false is, of course,

Christianity, but it is also education. Thus any educational institution that goes only so far is not really a Christian college; it is simply a college. This is a fine thing to be. But the problem of the curriculum in the Christian college is not the problem of truth and its free pursuit. Let no secular institution plead its " Christian " concern by parading its love of truth; let no Church-related school herald its " Christian" character by trumpeting its respect for knowledge.

Then what precisely is the nature of the problem for the Christian college? What is involved in order to make the curriculum a channel through which a Christian philosophy of education can flow to the students? This central question, I submit, has two aspects: first, it is a problem of the scope of information offered, and, secondly, it is a problem of the quality of atmosphere created in the classroom. As to the first, any college which seeks to be Christian must provide, among other things, for the study of the Hebrew-Christian tradition. It must be sure that adequate information concerning Christianity, its roots, its history, its multiform ramifications of thought and practice, is made available in the regular course of study. This is, by now, an old story; but its having been said in recent years with reiteration and force does not mean that such study is easy to provide. The difficulties attendant upon its incorporation in the curriculum justify our speaking of the matter as a problem. How can students best be introduced to a knowledge of Christianity?

### Courses in Christian Religion

One answer, of course, is that a specific area for such study should be established. If the college follows a departmental framework of organization, then there should be a department of religion, offering courses designed to acquaint the students with their religious heritage. If some divisional structure is pursued, then courses in religion can find their place among the humanities, probably in close association with offerings in philosophy. Here there is room for self-deception as to the proper role of the Christian college. Some institutions seem to believe that the point of departure should be some pleasantly neutral subject matter such as comparative religion, through which students can supposedly gain an overview with which they will then be better prepared to see their own Hebrew-Christian tradition. But we follow no such pseudotolerant scheme in the initial study of political science or literary masterpieces; we do not begin with comparative government or comparative literature. These things have their proper place in undergraduate offerings, and even so with comparative religion. But the point to begin is with our own heritage, that it be understood as clearly as possible; and the heart of the heritage is the Bible. The college that means to be Christian will offer its students a thorough study of the Old and New Testaments; and then will build upon that foundation courses in Christian history, theology, and ethics, and beyond those such other offerings in less crucial subject matter as the size and resources of the institution will allow.

A second answer, proceeding from the first and prompted by recent developments in educational theory, is to the effect that the study of religion should take its proper place in the college's program of general education. We have come a long way from President Eliot's system of free election, and all colleges have adopted, in less or greater measure, a core curriculum. It is difficult for even the secularists to exclude religion from a study of Western civilization or the classics of human thought. Christians will go secularists one better: they will find in the history of the Hebrew-Christian tradition and in Christian concepts of the nature of God and man the threads with which to bind the program of general education into some coherent whole.

It is with the third answer that the question of bootlegging sometimes arises. This position has it that religion should enter the curriculum by way of other disciplines, and some suspicious souls conclude that the intention is to drag religion into any and every subject, whether or not it fits. But such, of course, is not the correct meaning of the suggestion. Rather, the advice is to the effect that each course be taught fully and completely within its own sphere of subject matter; that only as religion is a legitimate part of that full treatment should it be included; but that, since it does happen to be so in numerous instances, its inclusion be undertaken in the normal teaching process. The Christian college, qua college, sticks to the task of teaching each discipline for what it is, no more; and the Christian college, qua Christian, knows that nearly every discipline depends upon information or insights drawn from the Christian tradition, and thus should be taught in recognition of this dependence, no less. Bootlegging is not involved. Religion should be included only when it legitimately inheres in the treatment of the subject.

Religionists have been saying such things for a number of years, but it often sounded like special pleading. Of late scholars in the various disciplines other than religion have raised their voices to similar effect. Historians realize that they teach the period of the Reformation only through knowing something about religion. Teachers of English literature know that an understanding of the writings of Milton or Browning or T. S. Eliot calls for a knowledge of religion. Political scientists concede that the Bill of Rights has religious rootage. And so it goes, from subject to subject. The Christian college will see to it that the subject matter of religion is present in the handling of every discipline in which it properly belongs.

A word needs to be said about the debate as to the relative merits of these various ways of including religion in the course of study. Some would have it that if we follow one method, then another is not necessary; if religion is included in the treatment of other subjects, then we need no separate courses in religion, or vice versa. But this is no either-or situation. On the contrary, the ubiquitous yet distinguishable nature of religion as a field of study and the all-inclusive character of education alike contend for a both-and approach. We need both religion in separate courses and material concerning religion in other courses, the former because there is a large body of knowledge and experience at the heart of our Western culture that goes under that name, and the latter because our understanding of other bodies of knowledge and experience is incomplete without reference to religion.

## MAJOR PROBLEMS

Once the college begins to attack this question of the scope of information about religion which is offered in its classrooms, certain subsidiary, yet very perplexing, problems emerge. We shall note four of them. First comes the ignorance of the students. All of us have our favorite stories of illustration. Yet this is not merely the usual illiteracy which is common also to other fields. This is worse: the presence of a large body of misinformation and misconception. Teachers in other areas, faced by ignorance, have at least merely a yawning vacuum to deal with. They can start from scratch, getting to work immediately on filling the vacuum. But teachers of religion must start before scratch; they must dig out a bed full of weeds before they can begin planting.

A second difficulty is the lack, in nearly every field, of textbooks that deal adequately with the relationship of religion to the subject matter under discussion. The wreckage of the irreligious years in higher education is still with us, often in the form of the texts which are used in countless courses across the country. That religion must have its full and proper place in the curriculum, in the various ways just described, is now being recognized more than ever before. But the textbooks still reflect the thinking of an earlier era, when secularism in education had its heyday. This danger too is being pointed out; but in the main the teacher still must rest pretty much on his own resources, with little help from the text, when he seeks to introduce material concerning religion at proper points in his teaching.

Yet this need to rely on his own knowledge and insight is the tip-off for the third special problem in this area, namely, the ignorance of teachers as well as of students. The average college teacher has woefully little to rely on. Like his students, he is full of misinformation and misconception, and sometimes, unlike his most inquiring students, he does not know it. This lack of realization of his own ignorance often shows itself as a kind of inverted fundamentalism, by which is meant that he labors under the notion that fundamentalism is all that religion has to offer, though he himself has rejected rather than accepted it on that account. But no matter whether he rejects or accepts the brand of religion he knows, the average teacher is tragically ill equipped to bring religion meaningfully into the classroom. At the moment we are concerned with the teacher's knowledge of religion, not his commitment — that will come later — and as far as his knowledge goes, he represents a tremendous barrier to the desire of the Christian college to introduce relevant information about religion into the curriculum.

Where are informed teachers to be found? Here we run into the fourth difficulty. The simple fact is that the programs of graduate study across the land are probably more secularized than any other one branch of higher education. And though graduate schools have long been castigated for their overspecialization, they have done little to change their ways. Secularization and specialization are the two tongue-twisting -izations that have produced most of our college teachers, and as long as they are in the saddle, there is little hope that we shall get the kind of teachers we need for the Christian colleges we envisage. Even in this dismal area, however, some light is beginning to shine; and if the Christian colleges will state their case with sufficient boldness, who knows? Maybe even our graduate schools will begin to listen.

## A Climate of Christian Concern

There is a second major aspect to the problem of the curriculum in the Christian college. The question of the scope of information offered is paralleled by the question of the quality of atmosphere created in the classroom. The challenge to introduce students to a knowledge of Christianity has as its counterpart the challenge to surround students with a climate of Christian conviction and concern. In each instance the latter as well as the former constitutes a specifically curricular problem as well as a more generalized aim for the Christian college as a whole.

I am aware that even the bare mention of such a proposition is enough to bring anathemas down upon one's head from all stripes of educators, from many self-confessed Christian teachers as well as from hardened secularists. We hear the sneers: Create an atmosphere? Surround students with a climate of Christian conviction and concern? Then the intention, after all, is propaganda, not education. The desirable products are " disciples," not independent scholars? If this is what it means to have a Christian curriculum, we want nothing of it. So run the objections of those who hear the idea for the first time and jump to easy but false conclusions. However, such fears are unfounded. We mean nothing that contradicts the accepted principles of good teaching and sound study. We have no desire to transform the classroom, either directly or insidiously, into a public forum or a sanctuary. Rather, we simply mean to focus more careful attention on what clear-sighted teaching and purposeful study really consist in, and on what actually goes on in a classroom as distinct from other types of gathering place. The Christian college will not forsake, but will be more conscious of, its role as a college when it becomes concerned with the general atmosphere of the institution.

Let us begin the analysis of this suggestion with some elementary considerations. What is the student doing? First of all, he is, presumably, learning. He acquires facts, and he receives interpretations of them. But this is not all. Up to this point he is simply receptacle; and our educational philosophies, of whatever school of thought, do not countenance any such limited notion of the student's status. Thus the word " learn " is stretched to include an active as well as a passive role — the student makes interpretations of his own, he learns by experience as well as by rote, he matures. But to say as much is to suggest that he is involved in a situation in which such a development on his part is encouraged — we want him to make interpretations of his own, to learn by experience, to mature. We make no apology for desiring to create in the classroom an atmosphere conducive to the maturing process. And when it exists, it *is* an atmosphere; it is something more than simply the stuff of information which the student is properly expected to acquire. Maturing is more than passive learning, and it takes place most readily, we know, when the climate is right.

And what about the teacher? What does he do? He gives facts, of course, he points out their interrelationships, and he describes various interpretations of them to which other scholars have come. Thus far his function may be said to be that of sharing the material of his subject matter. But he does not stop here because he cannot. He shares himself as well as his information. He lets the students know the nature of his own personal interpretations; and this he does either directly and honestly or indirectly and — yes, let us say it — dishonestly. These interpretations, overt or covert, inescapably carry him outside his own subject matter, whatever it is — and this is true even for the subject of religion — for they involve his general orientation in life, they stem ultimately from his world view. The teacher can no more hide such personal interpretations permanently from his students than he can hide a common cold, for they are part of his being a person. And his possessing them, and inevitably sharing them, sets a temper in his classroom, whether he intends it that way or no.

For example, let us take the case of a scientist who is also a thoroughgoing secularist. He follows the scientific method rigorously, let us suppose, and thus he shares with his students the results which such a method produces in his own discipline. He digs, he weighs, he measures, or he does whatever is appropriate to the materials with which he deals; and his students are called upon to learn the facts which he uncovers. But as a person as well as a scientist he not only follows the scientific method; he believes in it. If he is a good teacher, he succeeds in creating an atmosphere in his classroom that makes belief in it easy and attractive for his students. A secularist will probably go farther: he will believe that the scientific method is the sole avenue for arrival at truth, and perhaps by direction but quite often by innuendo he will suggest that the method of revelation is not to be countenanced.

When such a thing takes place, the teacher is sharing himself, that is, his philosophy of life, his world view, as well as his subject matter. His science is his content; his belief in science as alone valid is his personal philosophy. Whether or not all his students accept his belief, it sets the temper for the classroom just as surely as his choice of syllabus sets the content for the classroom.

The fact is clearly understood if we suppose that the scientist is a Christian. Such a teacher will use the scientific method as rigorously as his secularist colleague, and he too will believe in it. But he will also believe in something more. He will believe that man is not the measure of all things, that God has so made man as to be able to discover facts for himself, but that man is not limited in what he can know to what he himself has discovered. Man finds, but man is also apprised. God reveals himself in various ways, and has done so supremely in Jesus Christ. Intimations of God's revelation are present in the subject matter being taught and studied.

Such in general would be the position of the scientist who is a Christian. He is not called to preach this doctrine in every class session any more than the secularist is moved to expound his contrary dogma. But that he holds it, and expresses it frankly when it is pertinent to do so, affects the climate in which the students do their work. And the resultant atmosphere is entirely different from that which is created by the secularist.

## ATMOSPHERE AND PERSPECTIVE

All this has been referred to in recent educational writing as teaching from a perspective. Every person engaged in education teaches from some perspective, conscious or unconscious, mature or immature, Christian, sub-Christian, or non-Christian. It behooves the teacher to examine the perspective in which he does his work, the world view on the premises of which he goes about his daily chores. To underscore this necessity a host of books and pamphlets have been written in the last few years, many of them thoughtful and helpful, and conferences and seminars on such a theme have sprung up in all parts of the country. Supported by such agencies as the Danforth and Hazen Foundations, and by various educational groups, this emphasis has been pointed largely toward the proposition that a Christian perspective is of all others the soundest and most fruitful for higher education.

But in spite of the familiarity of this theme, I have not used the phrasing, "religious perspectives in college teaching," up to this point in my argument for two reasons: First, much of the discussion has to do, not so much with persepective, after all, as with content, the inclusion of the subject matter of religion in the teaching of other disciplines. Secondly, to center one's attention on the perspective of the teacher is to run the risk of losing the point of the discussion. The concern is not so much with the teacher's belief as it is with the climate of the classroom which that belief helps to mold. "Atmosphere" rather than "perspective" is the key word. This may be too fine a distinction for any use, but it is certainly true that the philosophical and religious orientation of the teacher is bound to affect the temper and spirit of the curriculum. For the Christian college this atmosphere must be Christian in its prevailing quality, and thus the personal testimony of the majority of its teachers must be Christian. Here indeed may be the most difficult aspect of the general problem of the curriculum in the Christian college.

Like the first major dimension of our problem having to do with the information offered in the curriculum, this second one dealing with the atmosphere in the classroom poses at least four subsidiary puzzlements which we must note briefly. First is the fear of even supposedly Christian folk to own to their commitments, coupled with the respect in educational circles for the god of objectivity. Yet this difficulty is not so great as it may seem at first glance. As to commitment, the parlous times in which we live are having at least the one good effect of making it clear that all men must take a stand for something; and the pose of pure objectivity not only is no longer fashionable in education but has been thoroughly unmasked as simply not tenable. Even that was a commitment, if to nothing more than the notion that commitment is not necessary. And so educators join with the rest of mankind in affirming the freedom and desirability that men, even teachers, should make conscious choice of their goals and their purposes, all the while achieving as large a measure of tolerance and fairness in their understanding of others' commitments as is possible for them.

That the choice of goals should be conscious leads to mention of the second danger. Unconscious subjectivity, representing unconfessed commitments, may be a continuing cancer in the work of the teacher even after the pretense of complete objectivity has been abandoned. Subjectivity will, of course, be present; the question is, What kind? Who is the safer guide for the students' maturing? The teacher who says, " Yes, I have some convictions, but I don't want to impose them upon the students," and then inevitably does so, at least in some measure, even when he does not intend it? Or the other teacher who says, " Since I cannot hide my beliefs altogether from my students, I will try to share them honestly, so that they may take conscious account of them in their own formulations "?

We should have no hesitation in choosing the second of these alternatives, if it were not for a nagging doubt that the teacher might use his rostrum for a soapbox. But I, for one, wish to protest. Why do we assume that the Christian teacher will force his belief on others, making its acceptance an illegitimate part of the requirements in the course, whereas the non-Christian will successfully escape such a temptation? The temptation must be escaped — let us not quibble on that point — for proselytizing is not education. But the Christian has at least as much protection, perhaps more, against such misuse of his function. For the Christian is usually more sensitive than the secularist to the distinction between his facts and his faith.

Here we become involved in the third special difficulty. This is the danger that the teacher will not discriminate, either in his own mind or for his students, between the two roles he must play in the classroom. He is scholar; he possesses knowledge. And he is person, or citizen, or man of faith; he possesses opinions and beliefs. When he faces his students, both the scholar and the citizen are present. But the danger is that he may play the second part when he thinks he is simply playing the first. That is, he may clothe his personal interpretations with the authority of his scholarship which of itself owns to no such interpretations. Thus the student receives the interpretation openly, and gets some inkling of the world view on which it is based — which is good; but he is also given the impression that these judgments are inherent in and essential to the course material — and that is bad.

Look at Gibbon's *Decline and Fall* or Kinsey's treatises on sexual behavior; or look through your eye of memory at many a teacher you have known. The fault is not that such folks have evaluated their material; and my complaint at the moment is not that their evaluations may differ from my own. Their fault, and my complaint, is that, blurring the point at which they pass from presentation to personal judgment, they make it appear that the opinions themselves are as authoritative as the material. Not simply as persuasive for the person himself — let it be so, for this is part of the substance of his faith — but as authoritative, as " scientific," if you will. The Christian and the secularist can both be guilty of this failure to distinguish between information and interpretation; and it is bad scholarship and bad teaching, no matter who does it.

If anything, the Christian is more guilty when it happens; but by the same token it is less likely to happen to him. For the Christian is by definition aware that the perspective from which he teaches comes from outside his subject matter and from outside all subjects in the curriculum, even religion as a subject of study. (Incidentally, one of the topics still to be considered by people writing in this field is the question of teaching religion from a religious perspective. It is not automatic, or universal; and especially in a Christian college religion as much as any other academic discipline deserves to be taught from a religious perspective.) The Christian teacher will own gladly to his faith when appropriate to the concerns of the class; he will label it as such, not hiding it, not forcing it, not confusing it with his factual material, and certainly not apologizing for it. In some such forthright fashion as this the integrity of both the students and the teacher will be better protected than through pseudo objectivity or ill-disguised indoctrination.

Now the Christian teacher may find that he wants to do more than simply state his case when it is proper to do so. Certainly the Christian college will want to make a greater impact on the student, on behalf of Christianity, than is appropriate throughout the curriculum alone. But — and here is the fourth difficulty — the teacher and the college must be on guard not to try to turn the classroom into a worship center. The other three dangers to the effort to make the climate of the curriculum sympathetic to Christianity constitute warnings that the atmosphere might easily be less sympathetic than it should or could be. This problem is just the opposite: the Christian college may be tempted to confuse the function of the teacher with that of the chaplain or director of religious activities. I for one am not at all sure that the Christian college should begin its classes with prayer.

## THE TEACHER AS WITNESS

But I am sure that the teacher's aim, as teacher, is not to convert in the sense of proselytize. Teaching from a Christian perspective means that the teacher will sooner or later testify in the classroom to his faith; but the reason for such testimony is that full information may be before the student, information both as to the subject and as to the teacher's interpretation of the subject in the light of his world view.

From the temper of the course the student can sense whether or not Christianity is essence, whether or not the teacher accepts the faith that life is more than meat, man is more than animal, God is more than man. The atmosphere of the classroom either supports such propositions or calls them in doubt, or even dismisses them. The teacher's statements help to form the atmosphere, but the teacher's actions, whether in consonance or discord with his statements, do so likewise. And again the spirit of the situation may actually run counter to the teacher's statements or actions if they should be out of harmony with the general temper of the college as a whole. For the whole college does have an atmosphere, and thus the whole curriculum can come to be influenced by it. In the college that has consciously adopted a Christian philosophy of education, the atmosphere of the classroom can be conducive to the student's thoughtful examination of Christianity as a live option of faith and practice for him.

The problems of the curriculum in the Christian college are one problem, how to translate a Christian philosophy of education into Christian curricular practice. This problem resolves itself into two major questions: first, whether the scope of information offered in the classroom includes information about Christianity in all relevant respects; and, secondly, whether the quality of atmosphere created in the classroom is characterized by Christian conviction and concern. To take those questions seriously is to push off on the path toward being a Christian college.

# 8

## MATERIALS AND METHODS IN THE CHRISTIAN COLLEGE

### *Ruth E. Eckert*

DURING the past three centuries the Christian college, which pioneered in the development of our program in higher education, has contributed incalculably to American life. Millions of students have left the campuses of our Church colleges deepened in their Christian commitment and prepared for effective service. Yet, the most convinced advocates of the Church college realize that it has often come far short of its high goals and that there are serious defects in much of what today is called Christian higher education. Possible ways of renewing and revitalizing the Christian college program are therefore being widely discussed and investigated. It is well that representatives of many different communions are participating in this effort, since the task ahead is a toilsome and varied one. It will demand the dedicated efforts of great numbers of co-workers to develop programs suited to the distinctive objectives of Christian higher education. Faced with today's uncommonly urgent problems, the Christian college cannot afford to be a second- or third-rate institution. It must demonstrate to a skeptical or hostile world the validity of the faith in which it has been founded.

### THE SETTING OF THE PRESENT PROPOSALS

Before exploring certain implications of our Christian faith for college teaching, particularly for the choice of instructional materials and methods, it may be well to sketch the setting for the present analysis.

Let us assume here a Christian liberal arts college of modest size and resources, and thus typical in these respects of hundreds of Church-related colleges and their programs throughout America, but differing markedly from those relying merely on nominal Church relationships or creedal profession to distinguish them from secular institutions. For this college is actively striving to be a Christian higher institution — to embody ever more fully in its programs and services those revealing insights which Christ alone provides. Because it has set high goals for itself as an institution of learning, it is first of all concerned with the recruiting and developing of a competent staff — persons of liberal learning, of scholarly interests, and of deep commitment to their task as Christian educators. Because it aims to afford students opportunities both for securing a sound liberal education and for developing their special interests and talents, it will seek to fashion an imaginatively conceived curriculum through years of study and experimentation. To implement its aims it must supply a broad program of testing and guidance, of student activities, of library and other auxiliary services. Finally, the college clientele will have to provide both the financial and spiritual support required to maintain the program at an effective level.

Turning now to the classroom, we take for granted that the teacher looks upon himself primarily as a guide, not as the chief actor or director; that he continually places the emphasis on students' learning, not on teaching per se, though as an instructor he has a skilled professional role to play. Instead of viewing his students as the objects of education, as persons to be educated, he regards them as the subjects of education, as active participants in the whole process. Recognizing the fact that learning is an intensely personal affair, something that each individual must ultimately achieve for himself, the teacher functions chiefly as a stage setter and scene-shifter, described so well in Marie Rasey's provocative volume *This Is Teaching*.[1] His aim throughout is not to support or to exalt himself but to maximize his students' intellectual competence, emotional independence, and spiritual growth.

While effective college teaching demands scholarly competence in both the subject matter to be taught and the sociopsychological disciplines to be practiced, it remains primarily an art. Each teacher must strive to develop his own style and technique suited to his abilities, personality, and background, as well as to his particular objectives and students. Thus when he decides to introduce some new materials, he will normally re-examine the methods he has been using; similarly, as he tries different methods, he will require some adjustment in classroom materials.

However, it must be stated at this point that college teachers have typically not given the question of instructional materials and methods the attention it deserves. As Umstattd's recent inquiry into college teaching procedures shows, most college teachers tend to rely heavily on one or two approaches.[2] Though they could use an almost endless variety of learning experiences, they too often limit their students' activities to listening to the professor and to reading books. Nor have college instructors always been too clear-sighted as to what they hope to gain from the processes of teaching and learning. After visiting hundreds of classes throughout the country, Dr. Paul Klapper, the former president of Queens College, identified, as his most overwhelming impression, the aimlessness of much college instruction. Neither teachers nor students seemed to know very well what ends they were seeking.[3] Yet only when they have squarely faced and resolved the problem of goals are faculty members able to make a discriminating selection of means for promoting those goals. The more sharply focused objectives become, the greater the likelihood of their realization through instruction. The importance of examining closely the major meanings of the Christian faith for our task as educators may not be underestimated.

## SOME GUIDING PRINCIPLES

For our ideal Christian college let us examine six propositions fundamental in the selection of all materials and methods of instruction. They have been developed around a few beliefs that appear central to the Christian view of man and the world and are intended to underscore a few of our primary concerns as Christian educators dealing with materials and methods useful to the imaginative teacher in promoting his ends.

1. The dignity and worth of each individual are stressed, and responsibility is accepted for promoting his fullest development, intellectually, socially, and spiritually.

Though concern for this objective is shared by some non-Christians, it reaches its full meaning only in the context of God as Redeemer as well as Creator. Because the Christian college program is viewed to be more fundamental and purposeful than one serving merely as a steppingstone to vocational or social advancement, teachers will do everything in their power to cultivate insight into and appreciation of man's common humanity. The fact that the Son of God became the Son of Man to raise men to full membership in the family of God will confer upon good teaching in this faith a depth of meaning that the secularist cannot hope to achieve. The concept of man's worth can then become one of the great themes in general education courses, so that students gain insight into man and society, not just into the preliminaries of specialized work. In the light of this proposition wide use will be made of our humanistic traditions — the great literature, art, music, and philosophy of our own and other cultures — as a help not only in understanding history or in developing aesthetic appreciations but in grasping the meaning of such primary values as human dignity, moral responsibility, and freedom of the will. These ideas will also receive attention in classes in political science, philosophy, economics, psychology, education, and other fields, where students will be encouraged to discuss and define them for themselves. In other words, the whole program of general and liberal education will be designed to develop a sound understanding of what it is to be a man, that is to say, to understand man's anxieties, insecurities, and despair, as well as his strivings and aspirations, and how, in the new humanity which Christ came to establish, man can become what he most deeply craves to be.

Along with this emphasis on our common humanity will go an equally well-defined stress on the irreplaceability of the individual — that he is, to quote Ralph Harper, a " once-for-all being " in the world.[4] Individuality will be promoted by giving students plenty of elbowroom to develop in distinctive ways. By allowing considerable latitude in the choice of materials and projects, teachers will encourage each student to develop his characteristic talents and proclivities. Perhaps college faculty members have been too ready to encourage conformity to their own views, seeking to produce imitations of themselves rather than persons who differ from them and even come to differ more notably than when they first came under instruction. Several recent studies indicate that college teachers usually do observe intellectual and cultural diversities, but do not sufficiently consider and include special interests, goals, and personality patterns. Thus, Lauren Wispe, in appraising several teaching methods used in social relations courses at Harvard, found that, whereas the introspective or "inner-directed" students profited more from classes in which the professor gave a good deal of structuring to the sessions, students who were more outgoing and at ease in social situations did their best work in a quite relaxed, permissive type of class.[5] An interesting study by Maas suggests that the teacher's own personality will also determine how successfully he can use the so-called "instructor-centered" or "student-centered" approaches.[6] Class experiences should be planned so that learners come to accept and appreciate differences among their colleagues. By affording each student a sense of unforced acceptance and security, the teacher helps him to develop both self-insight and a respect for individuality in other people.

2. The search for truth and the quests of Christian idealism can thrive only when searchers are free to inquire, to discuss, to compare, and to make their own choices. Only where searchers are free will freedom be generally cherished and protected.

Because the Christian college prizes freedom, it helps its members to enter into their full heritage of liberty. In many different courses the explorers of learning are confronted with the great writings about human freedom and encouraged to discuss and to analyze them, so that they may discover for themselves how firmly rooted many of our teachings are in the Hebraic-Christian view of man. Situations in which freedom is being currently challenged are likewise openly discussed, not only in class but with presidents, deans, and trustees, who, when courageously supporting their faculty's efforts, can stimulate thoughtful study of controversial issues. No problem, in fact, will be considered out of bounds for responsible investiga-tion by teachers and students in the Christian college. Since academic freedom is conceived, not as the prerogative of professors alone, but as broad intellectual freedom, students will be encouraged to question prevailing views, including those of the instructor and even those of the institution itself. Recognizing that sincere questions are the first necessary step toward fuller understanding, teachers will be concerned not so much about students who express honest doubts as about those who seem to experience no real problems intellectually in reconciling their faith with their growing knowledge. A free flow of ideas will likewise be promoted by letting students know that many of their teachers are still struggling with grave intellectual problems. Instructors who give pat answers to questions that have continued to baffle thoughtful men are hardly likely to stimulate anyone to new levels of maturity and insight.

Disclosures from some recent investigations, probing student at-titudes toward instruction, are somewhat disquieting here. Though we like to think of a college as pre-eminently a place where eager young minds are engaged in freely examining and criticizing ideas, yet we are apprised that students characteristically think they do not get much practice in such pursuits. While they express favorable opinions about their teachers, they tend to rate highest the items that emphasize the instructor's own competence and activity. For ex-ample, students usually feel that their teachers have a quite thorough knowledge of their subject, that they prepare themselves well for their classes and make clear, explicit assignments. But much lower is their rating in items inquiring whether these same instructors en-courage them to think for themselves. For example, in only forty of some three hundred and sixty Arts College classes studied on our own University of Minnesota campus did the typical student indicate that much original thinking had been expected.[7] Studies made in many other institutions, including Church-related colleges, support this conclusion. Perhaps this circumstance explains why eight hun-dred and twenty college presidents and deans, who were recently given an opportunity to specify traits that they felt should be em-phasized in the selection and preparation of college teachers, gave first rank to " the ability to inspire students to think for themselves." [8]

The lecture-recitation methods used in most classrooms may be significantly related to these apparent defects. Dr. Benjamin Bloom, for example, who has analyzed the thought processes of students during lectures and group discussions, discovered that the lecture method was especially successful " in securing the attention of students to what is being said, but that it evoked primarily those thoughts that are appropriate to the following and comprehending of information," while the discussion was more successful in evoking " complex problem-solving types of thought." [9] In fact, he found that the least efficient discussion was superior to most lectures in this latter respect.

The instructional program in the Christian college will, of course, be set up in such a way as to make evident the fact that " free " thought has some conditions. Students will be helped, through actual analysis of their own experiences and those of other people, to see that sin and fear can so distort men's perceptions and warp their judgments that they cannot analyze problems clearly. Only as Christ breaks the thralldom of these internal states, so that men become progressively released from self-centeredness, do they really become free and independent human beings, able to see and to study the world as it is. Part of Christ's great statement, " The truth shall make you free," cannot therefore properly be appropriated, as many secular groups attempt to do, without accepting the other breathtaking half, " I am the truth." Students must also be helped to establish for themselves the fact that freedom does not mean irresponsibility. As freedom to investigate and to think increases, responsibility for action becomes correspondingly greater. Though growing knowledge may set bounds as to what individuals can properly do, it never releases them from the moral imperative to put their new insight to fruitful use. In fact, if freedom does not lead to such decision and commitment, it becomes an empty and barren concept. As Ralph Harper states, " Freedom and passionate commitment are not incompatible: one without the other is actually enslavement." [10]

3. The primacy of faith is acknowledged, and the fact recognized that man must accept and live by values that can never be wholly validated experimentally.

In the Protestant view, faith and knowledge are not opposed,

though faith normally transcends what can be established on purely
rational or empirical grounds. Just as the great Reformed doctrine of
justification by faith — when it is properly understood — leads, not
to a disregard of good works but to more consecrated Christian living, so the principle of the primacy of faith actually gives deeper
meaning to intellectual activity. Though Protestants admit that human reason must be guided and corrected by divine revelation, they
do not minimize the significance of man's rational powers. Convinced that even redeemed men know only in part and that they
apprehend imperfectly, Protestant Christians have felt impelled to
strip away as completely as they can the fetters of ignorance, bias,
and downright sin that dim men's view. Hence, they have advocated
the widest possible diffusion of educational opportunities, with each
individual afforded as much schooling as his abilities warrant. Sound
scholarship has also been deeply venerated and the search for new
knowledge encouraged on the widest possible front.

How can students, through their classroom experiences, gain some
realization of the importance of this Reformed principle? Perhaps, in
the first place, teachers can marshal experiences that will help them
to glimpse that it is not only in the realm of religion that faith is so
crucial. They need to see that bold venturing in the form of educated
guesses precedes fruitful study in almost any field. Both in theory-
building and in empirical investigations the formulation of hypoth-
eses must be the initial step, guiding and giving direction to further
study. Likewise in human relationships, faith and mutual trust build
an atmosphere conducive to creative discovery. Talents are released,
for example, not so much by teachers who know many facts regarding individual differences, important though such information is, as
by those whose confidence and high expectation can stimulate others
to realize their potentialities.

By affording students considerable practice in firsthand study of
problems, instructors can help them to understand the possibilities
and limits of the empirical approach. Not those who have merely
been told about scientific methods of attack and think they are expected to copy solutions that others have devised, but those who have
themselves struggled to reach acceptable conclusions will appreciate

keenly the assumptions the scientist initially makes and how they shape his investigation. Such inquirers will also recognize how partial and variable their data often are, and in how far they may or may not serve in the selecting and critcizing of means and in making sound value-judgments. They will see, in other words, that faith and knowledge are essentially complementary, each playing its distinctive role, but both serving in God's plan to stimulate and develop the human personality.

4. The right and duty of private judgment are emphasized, with each individual held accountable primarily to God for the quality of his decisions.

Since the Christian college seeks to foster reflective commitment, it will continuously confront its learners with issues, choices, and challenges, with the questions that men cannot dodge if they are to act intelligently. They will therefore not be allowed to take comfortable refuge in the watered-down answers set forth in texts or in the instructor's own neat resolutions of trying problems. Instead, they will be expected to study independently and to reach their own conclusions. Such direct experiences with conflicting views should help them to develop some appreciation; to use William Hocking's telling phrase, it is the " tug of the contest " from which significant choices have emerged.[11] " Case methods " of teaching, if widely employed, will enable more liberal arts instructors and those teaching in professional fields to bring vivid cross sections of life into the classroom, so that serious searchers may grapple with real problems. The several applications given in Sidney French's recent book *Accent on Teaching* are richly suggestive of such possibilities.[12]

Evidences from another recent study, dealing in this instance with undergraduate use of the library, raises some disturbing questions as to whether college teaching encourages as much active drive for solutions as we should like to believe. Investigations have found that most students go to the library to consult specifically assigned books or articles, not to find relevant materials for themselves.[13] They seem to be getting scant practice in locating source materials, evaluating them, and using the same with wisdom and discrimination, skills they will almost certainly need in their out-of-school years.

Because the Christian teacher looks toward translating knowledge, belief, and values into better patterns of living, he will emphasize in his classwork the application of new learnings. Glib answers on tests cannot be accepted as evidence either that the student has acquired functional skills and abilities or that he will be motivated to use them productively. Passive, hurried absorption of the written or spoken word will therefore be discouraged in favor of personal reflection, interpretation, and use of these learnings. Informal discussions, panels, sociodramas, case studies, laboratory exercises of new design, individually guided reading projects, and dozens of other approaches can be employed to provoke an examination of problems and an exercising of convictions.

Though our Protestant tradition has stressed the values of independence for individuals and for small bodies of men, we have not always put such independence into effective practice in the college classroom. Too often, even in our Christian colleges, work is so excessively supervised that it fails to develop any real sense of self-direction. In days when totalitarianism, whether of the Fascist, Communistic, or ecclesiastical varieties, constitutes a more deadly threat than the hydrogen bomb, the Christian college teacher should be a great helper in understanding all aspects of our heritage. Opportunities should be provided not only for studying thoroughly the writings that have nurtured democracy in both Church and State but also for gaining varied experiences in democratic living. This means much more than allowing some form of student government on the campus, usually limited to the extracurricular phases of the college program; it means, rather, using every classroom as a kind of laboratory for learning how to live and work with other human beings. It does not imply surrendering the professional role of the teacher, leaving students free to do as they please, even at the cost of considerable fumbling, but it does mean co-operative working and planning for the fruitful uses of time in class and associated activities, followed by a constant appraising of how successful these efforts have been. Students should thus be educated for responsible service in their local churches and communities and on the broader front of state, nation, and world.

One critical problem that the teacher faces in this connection lies in the great pressures toward conformity that today affect students as well as their elders. Experimental studies by Asch,[14] Schacter,[15] and others show how formidable this pressure is, and how, for many individuals, it will outbalance the clear weight of evidence supporting a different position. Christian teachers would seem to have a special responsibility for protecting the expression of minority views. To quote Dettering's recent article, they must " work within the new democratic group process to establish the sanctity of dissent." [16] For a student to re-echo an orthodox interpretation merely because it is his teacher's view or the one accepted on his campus may augur far less for his future testimony and service than if he maintained with considerable courage and reason some position which is not so widely understood or favored by his colleagues. If teachers really want to cultivate such responsible individual study and decision, they must guard against every unthinking adoption of prevailing views. In fact, the conscientious teacher must at times play the role of the opposer or challenger, to keep his students from assenting to a position that does not stem from their own honest belief and conviction.

5. The realization of God's purpose is sought not only in individual lives or in the Church but in the whole society of men.

In programs with a genuinely Christian social orientation, students will come early to understand the concept of brother's keeper, a view that takes on its full meaning only when God is recognized as Father. The controlling purpose will be to help each individual to develop a virile Christian ethic and apply it resolutely in his personal and social relationships, despite possible hostility and ridicule.

A broad social outlook can be promoted in a variety of ways, beginning in the classroom, where co-operative practices will replace many highly competitive ones. Though the Christian view has always emphasized men's social interdependence, which is the principle that individuals develop best in a society of fellows, it has been seriously neglected in much of our teaching. Too often responsibilities have been conceived in terms of meeting the instructor's requirements, not of contributing significantly to other members of their learning group. In fact, many of them are often so preoccupied individually with trying to predict what the professor expects of them that they do not get on to their real business of learning.[17] In the truly Christian college, students will sense from the outset that they are obligated, not just to their teachers, but to their fellows. Tasks, for example, can be set up so that numerous individual and small-group projects that have issued from the classroom will, in turn, contribute to larger undertakings.

If students are not to join the swelling ranks of the drifters or indifferentists on social questions, the Christian college itself must be more than a world-removed institution existing in a kind of monastic seclusion. Rather, its staff and students, involved in a variety of off-campus studies and services, must be determined to keep its program vitally related to the problems that men and women face in our world today. Some of the materials and experiences utilized in class projects will be designed to aid in understanding underprivileged and rejected peoples, so that students may come to realize, in some measure, the injustices and inequities, the misery, sin, and suffering that still haunt human existence. Nor will instructors shrink from having them assess the Church's lacks, dealing realistically with our frequent failures as Protestant Christians to take a strong stand on questions of social justice and human freedom. Wisely chosen community studies and work experiences will not only enrich general education but should also build a compelling sense of Christian obligation to right wrongs.

6. God, as revealed in Christ, is regarded as the ultimate ground of faith and hope, and therefore as the true end of the educational process.

Teaching, like every other aspect of the Christian college program, will not find its focal point in the student, in society, or in the particular subject matter, important though all these will be in any soundly conceived plan of instruction. Instead, it will discover its true meaning in Christ, who is seen as central not only in the Scriptures but in history and in individual Christian experience. All other aims of Christian education will thus become subordinate to this Christ-centered one. Adapting Lewis Mumford's telling figure, such a cen-

tral affirmation, like a magnet, " will continuously polarize each frag-
ment that enters the field, giving knowledge and experience far
deeper meaning than they would otherwise have had." [18] Were the
view taken of Christ a low or narrow one, it might have a restricting
influence on an educational program. But the concept of the transcendent, yet immanent God, who became incarnate in Christ,
should stimulate teachers and students alike to search for larger
meanings and to bring their lives into ever closer conformity with
them.

What effect might this final principle have on teaching and learning in the Christian college? Would the staff develop this concept
only through courses in religion and philosophy? Or would students
be encouraged in every course to look for more ultimate meanings, to
be alert to " intimations of the divine " in the physical universe about
them, in human relationships, in the revealed Word, and in the quiet
of their own hearts? Might they be challenged to think about God's
ways in history and contemporary life, looking for an " infinite dimension " in every problem and circumstance of man's life? Courses
in all areas of liberal education would thus seek not to indoctrinate
but to cultivate " ultimate concern for the Ultimate " which, according to Paul Tillich, constitutes the very heart of religion.

Christian college teachers might nurture this search for more final
and satisfying answers in many ways, but principally by spurring
students to think for themselves, to study thoughtfully the Old and
New Testament writings which constitute our primary sources for
understanding God and man, to become soundly based in the disciplines that illumine man's experiences, and to develop a personal philosophy that embodies their deepest beliefs and values. Part of this
nurturing can be done in regular courses; it can also be encouraged
through reading projects, in tutorial conferences, and in senior-in-
tegrating seminars followed by comprehensive examinations. Many
opportunities to relate, to reflect, and to integrate present themselves for cultivating perspective or a kind of synoptic view. Their
fuller utilization might meet undergraduates' frequent criticism that
teachers seldom afford experiences designed to relate new learnings
to other course work or to out-of-school living. Under such stimulat-

ing instruction more and more learners should move from concern for trivialities and unrelated particulars to a world of wholes. The fragmentation and specialization which have so often distorted undergraduate programs can be increasingly obviated in institutions cultivating a sense of unity and Christian purpose. Thus the ultimate test of all materials and methods must be found in the quality of the insights, action, and Christian commitment developed by the students. To grasp this thought is to appreciate, in some measure at least, how great is the mission of the truly Christian college.

# 9

## ADMINISTRATION IN THE CHRISTIAN COLLEGE

### O. P. Kretzmann

THERE can be no doubt that there are problems of administration
in a Christian college. Some of them are shared with schools
under the secular orientation, and others are specifically ours. My
observations are somewhat negatively colored by the fact that I spent
my first ten years in the educational world as an instructor. During
those quiet and happy years I learned to view all administrators with
a jaundiced eye. There were some who had an unquiet and unhappy
way of intruding upon the warm, intimate relationship between
teacher and student which is really the heart of all true education. In
fact, I have long been persuaded that administration in all colleges is
vastly overemphasized. There are two areas in American education
that need de-emphasis in our time and generation. The first is inter-
collegiate athletics, and the second is administration. Both can tend,
inevitably and tragically, to become leviathans that crush the living,
vital essence of education. It has often seemed to me that by a subtle
osmosis from the business and industrial world the American college
and university has acquired a philosophy of administration that
may be necessary for Sears Roebuck and International Harvester but
is almost deadly when it is used in the halls of ivy. The administrator
becomes the boss, the chief, the employer; the teacher becomes the
employee; and the student becomes the product, numbered, pack-
aged, and neatly delivered at the end of the assembly line with a
hundred and twenty credits and a hundred and twenty quality
points, sometimes more but never less. The instructor, who is really

the heart of the matter, does a competent job from 9:00 A.M. to 3:00 P.M. and then returns to his easy chair and his garden, hoping that the administration will give him an increase in wages and a raise in rank the following academic year. The corrosive effect of the situation on a profession which must be free, adventurous, and bold in order to be great can hardly be overestimated.

This is one of the reasons why some of the recent witch hunts for Communists on our college and university faculties were so ridiculous. Our real problem is not the rare, almost nonexistent, noncomformist who occasionally explores an intellectual, social, or spiritual blind alley. He is soon discovered and brought back to the fold or cast into outer darkness. Far more subtly dangerous for a living democracy and a vital, adventurous Christianity on our campuses is the academic Caspar Milquetoast, the timid, fearful teacher who lives in dread of administrative disapproval and a summons from the office of the president. We would do well, I truly believe, to examine our entire philosophy of administration at our colleges and universities with a coldly critical and disapproving eye. We, and our faculties, are victims of a historical devolution which threatens to destroy our heritage of freedom and greatness under God.

Perhaps it is desirable for us to view this entire problem more historically than we have in the immediate past. In his volume *Christian Education in a Democracy,* Professor Frank E. Gaebelein, the headmaster of the Stonybrook School, writes:

‘ The earliest colleges and universities were more democratic than is generally realized, for students and faculty were in complete charge. However, as the work grew, administrative posts developed; much as the Early Church appointed deacons to free the apostles from ‘ serving tables,’ so the colleges appointed deans to allow the faculty to devote themselves to teaching and research. But bureaucracy is a subtle thing, and today ‘ Deans Within Deans,’ the title of one of Jacques Barzun’s essays, is too accurate to be wholly facetious. The answer to overorganization is to revive the concept of a college as a community of scholars and students in which the administration sees faculty members, not as mere employees, but as trusted participants in policy-making " (p. 150).

The problem becomes even more glaringly evident when we compare our American approach to administration with the European, both English and Continental, manner of conducting the affairs of an academic community. In a recent address before the faculty of the University of Chicago, Chancellor Kimpton reported on a journey to Europe, which deserves to be cited here at some length:

"The first thing that struck me was that nobody — and I mean nobody — knew or even cared who the head of his institution was. Very often the vice-chancellor or the rector or whoever presumably provided the leadership for the institution was an innocent scholar elected from the faculty who unwillingly carried the loathsome burden and unloaded it the first moment possible. Upon the whole I found this disturbing. I had come to think of the president of a university as a person who held a high and mighty office and who was expected to provide educational leadership of a lofty and innovating kind. It was the gentle rector of Lyon, I believe, who asked me in this connection if I had ever heard of the head of the University of Paris in the twelfth century when it provided the intellectual leadership that brought the Western world from the Dark Ages. And Oxford and Berlin have provided equally profound leadership at crucial points in the development of our civilization, and who were the vice-chancellors or rectors at these turning points? They have passed like the snows of yesteryear and the monumental contribution in retrospect was not made by them at all but rather by a faculty who dared think in new and alarming ways to produce a different world. It was even suggested by citizens of the countries that had known Fascism that it is a dangerous thing to have a *Führer,* to superimpose a pattern of thought and behavior upon a people. And if it is dangerous for a nation, it is even more so for a university. Perhaps the only role of administration is to provide the context in which the genius of a faculty can develop and flourish. The administrator has two functions, and though they are important, they are certainly limited. He must interpret the university to and defend the university against the world which lies beyond its walls; and within the university he must stand watch over its intellectual quality. He needs the courage and conviction to weather the squalls of ephemeral public and even faculty sentiment; he ought to be able to make a persuasive case for his university in a public place; and he should possess the guile to lure money from the surprisingly few people and organizations that have it. If the European model has anything to suggest, it is that the great head of a great university is really not great at all. His only job is to gather together a great faculty, protect, pay, and interpret them, and then leave them alone. If he has succeeded, everybody is aware of the stature of his institution and nobody has ever heard of him.

" But this was only the first of a series of shocks that I received. It is a shocking thing for an American to observe that money, and even the things that money buys, like salaries and facilities, do not matter very much. The unskilled laboring man in America receives more than a professor in France, who, it is assumed, will hold professorships in several institutions or have some outside job in order to make ends meet. I don't mean to suggest for an instant that the French professor likes this arrangement, but it still is the case that the French universities are distinguished, and they continue to draw to them extremely able young people who desire a life of research and teaching. There is nothing much left physically of the German universities, but it is amazing what an ingenious fellow can do with a pencil and a piece of paper. I was particularly impressed with the fact that remarkable scientific work can go on without the proliferation of apparatus and big machines and big scientific buildings. Our Government in a burst of generosity had just offered to pacific Western nations some radioactive isotopes and instruction on the mysteries of big reactors and cosmotrons. The European scientists with whom I talked were curiously un-

interested. They thought they knew about as much as we did
without going through the laborious construction of gadgets."

It is evident from all this that I believe that the Christian college
in America should take the lead in de-emphasizing the importance
of administration. Many functions now conducted by presidents and
deans should be returned to our faculties. The Christian college is in
a uniquely fortunate position to do this. Our relation to our teaching colleagues is not as employer to employee, nor even as partners
in a great and common enterprise. It is much higher and greater and
deeper than that. It is in Christ. We are partners in God, fellow
members of the body of Christ, the communion of saints. It is evident, therefore, that the relation of administration of a Christian
college to the faculty and students must be vastly more human and
personal than in schools that are not under the light of the cross.
It must be authentically and consistently Christian. It must work person to person. Efficiency can be only a partial goal. It must be hori-
zontal rather than vertical, nurturing a sense of community in Christ,
a warmth and affection that have their roots in the giving and desiring love of the living God as he has come to us in the person of
Jesus Christ.

We have need, therefore, of a theology of administration. In fact,
in the practical and immediate view, this may be our most pressing
and crying problem and our greatest opportunity to bring something
new and fresh and great to the American educational system. While
it is always difficult to translate a spiritual relationship into academic
terms, it must be done if our Christian colleges are to retain their
historic character and make a distinctive contribution to American
education.

It is evident from the foregoing that, barring our elimination of
the administration, the first and greatest task of the administration
of a Christian college is internal. It lies in its relation to the faculty
and the student body, in the firm establishment of a living community in which all relationships will be determined by the spirit and
power of the gospel. When these purposes are translated into immediately practical terms, some of the specific approaches may be

very similar to those used at schools with a non-Christian orientation. It should always be remembered, however, that the motivation
is totally different and that therefore some of the methods will also
differ markedly.

In their relationship to the faculty all administrators should strive
to give their teaching staff physically a sense of quiet security and intellectually a sense of adventurous security. Physically and financially
this means adequate salaries, good housing, an intelligent system
of tenure, and a strong retirement program. The limits of these four
objectives will, of course, be determined by the varying circumstances
in which individual institutions find themselves. Some of us have
more money than others. In all cases, however, the faculty should
know that the administration is doing the very best it can for them,
and that the best hours of the day and the lonely hours of the night
are devoted to their welfare.

If I may be permitted to choose one of these points for further elaboration, I would turn to the retirement program. This is perhaps
the most important point in our concern for our instructional staffs.
All of them know that their salaries will never equal the wages of a
business executive, a salesman, or even the carpenter who repairs
their front porch. If, however, they can know that their years of
diminishing returns and declining strength have received our af-
fectionate attention, many of their worries will be ended. Since their
intelligence is higher than the average, they think more sharply and
sensitively of the long, and yet brief, years ahead. They want to know
what will happen to them, their wives, and their children when the
shadows lengthen and the hour grows late. If we can demonstrate
that we share their concern, practically and intelligently, they will
respond with a loyalty and a devotion to the cause of Christian
higher education which can make our schools lighthouses of community and fortresses of united strength.

Intellectually, I believe it is the task of an administrator to give the
faculty a sense of adventurous security. This means that no one in
the constituency should be permitted to attack an individual member of our teaching staffs directly. All criticism must come to the administration. In many cases this is one of the most important tasks

of a sound administration. Our teachers must be given freedom under the general philosophy and theology of the school which they serve. This freedom is, of course, something totally different from the various forms of license that have occasionally been dignified under the term " academic freedom " in the twentieth century. Freedom in a Christian college is the freedom with which Christ has made us free, the liberty of the children of God. It is immediately defined and outlined by the reborn nature of the men and women who have it. I believe that the concept of " academic freedom " can be worked out much more easily at a Christian college than anywhere else. It is the great, eternal freedom to do what God wants us to do, rather than what we want to do.

The atmosphere of community can also be created by such technical means as frequent meetings of the faculty and a faculty lounge. The latter, it seems to me, is more significant than the former. Faculty meetings can often be monopolized by brethren who are more vocal than eloquent, and more articulate than relevant. On the other hand, the informal gathering with coffee can often be exceedingly valuable in answering questions, developing some embryonic ideas, or giving the neophyte a chance to fight. Closely allied to this approach is the open-door policy of the dean and the president. They should be available just as much as possible, in spite of the crazy-quilt arrangement of time under which presidents, especially, live and move. I have also found that it is very much worth-while to become a peripatetic administrator at least once a week. If I remember correctly, this practice was instituted at Harvard by President Eliot. If an administrator can find one afternoon a week to wander aimlessly around the campus and talk to a member of the faculty who is strolling across the green, to the students who are finishing their three o'clock class, to maintenance men who are cutting the lawn, he will be a wiser and better man. These are the people who make up the life and work of a college. To know them, to be interested in their problems, is an essential part of the task of the administrator. It gives them a sense of belonging.

Finally the administrator of a Christian college should do everything possible to give the members of his faculty a definite sense of

progress. Here too a thoroughly Christian theology of education con-
nects this entire process with the progress of sanctification in the individual. The recognition of the fact that an instructor is doing a
better job before God and man this year than last year is very important to him and to his entire development. Some of us have found
that little notes of encouragement to members of the faculty at fairly
regular intervals, particularly at contract time, the weeding and
winnowing of the academic world, can really accomplish much in
giving them this needed sense of progress. It is evident, of course,
that grants-in-aid for graduate study, an established plan of promo-
tion, and the paying of expenses to meetings of learned societies
must be a part of the administration of any good Christian college.
Perhaps it should be said again that all these methods and techniques
are quite meaningless unless they are adopted in the spirit of Christ.
This means again that the motivating power behind anything that
we do for our teaching staff must be our love for Christ and our
love for them in Christ.

The relationship of the administration to the student body is of
equal importance. In fact, some administrators would put it in first
place. It is evident, of course, that deans of student affairs, directors
of residence halls, and counselors must remain close to the life and
thought of the students. This sounds very trite, but it is astonishing
to note how often it is forgotten in the routine of paper work, of dis-
ciplinary cases, and of setting up a maze of rules and regulations
which make the relationship between the administration and the
student a perpetual and futile game of " hide-and-seek " or even of
" cops and robbers." If this approach would end only in the curious
legends which alumni gifted with an imaginative memory recount
at home-coming, one could possibly overlook the whole business.
Unhappily, however — even tragically — it often results in our failure
to develop good traits of character and in the distortion of the concepts of authority, discipline, responsibility, and freedom. Since these
are all essential in the sound working of a democratic society and a
functioning Church, the Christian college may well need to look
again at its work in the field of student relations. Must it be said
that in this area some of our colleges are not very Christian? They

seem to operate as though there never had been a New Testament. Sinai supplants Calvary. The freedom of the Christian man, the relationship of the Law and the Gospel, the God-given redeemed dignity of the individual Christian under the grateful response to the cross, all these are forgotten in an abortive effort either to be like unchristian schools or to cultivate the atmosphere of concentration camps.

Fundamentally our essential problem in the area of student affairs is the maintenance, consciously and consistently, of the delicate balance between freedom and responsibility. This is admittedly very difficult. It requires, first of all, a clear concept of the nature of ultimate authority, an unswerving loyalty to the indicatives and imperatives of the divine Word. The administration of a Christian college can have no illusions about the nature of man. It must insist on the reality and gravity of sin and the equal reality and glory of the atonement. It can have no fear of the life of the mind because it gladly submits the mind of man to the mind of God. It can never confuse freedom with license because it recognizes the great fact that the last freedom of the human heart and mind is in God — in the liberty wherewith Christ has made us free. This approach, it seems to me, is the only one that is Biblically realistic and finally permanently valid. It will be noted that in the life of the individual it revolves around the concepts of sin and grace. Under the concept of sin it sees the student clearly and realistically. Under the concept of grace it brings God into the life of the student. In this way it has an almost incredibly powerful approach to the fundamental problems of the search for truth, of education in the highest sense of the word, and in the establishment of the relevance of the Christian gospel to all areas of human life and thought. Consistently followed through, this approach to the problems of the student body can bring magnificent results for the world of tomorrow. There is a hard core of changelessness in our Western civilization which must be brought sharply to the attention of the individual student. Because we have forgotten that truth and have been cut by the acids of modernity and have developed, even in Christian colleges, a cult of uncertainty, we are now so afraid and alone in a world that has suddenly moved beyond our power to control it. It is only through a very real and thoughtful approach to the doctrine of man that we can begin to rebuild the ruined temples of our society.

Concerning the other tasks of the administration of a Christian college I shall say very little. All administrators must be fund raisers, public relations experts, commencement speakers, and members of our service clubs. This is especially true of presidents. Deans may occasionally be unsocial, unhappy, and unlovely, but not presidents. They must be masters of the hearty handshake, the cheery smile, the good word. Under these circumstances it is amazing to note that so many of them are still good and noble and deeply Christian men.

More seriously, however, there are certain specific areas beyond the campus walls in which the administration of a Christian college has special problems and duties. One of them, in which all others are included, is the maintenance of an honest and consistent relationship with the constituency of the college. Here too we have often failed. We have said one thing and done another. It is probably true that a Christian college can never be a perfect mirror of all the ideas, traditions, and prejudices of its constituency. If it tries, it will soon turn from a clouded mirror into a chameleon. Its task, therefore, is to take from the Church those traditions and ideas that are permanently and distinctively valid and to translate them into educational practice. A truly Christian college often finds that it is the burning focal point of all the problems and tensions within its constituency. The tumult of the Church and the world becomes the turmoil of the campus. We should expect that. Only in this way can we separate the wheat from the chaff, the permanent from the temporary, the eternal from the momentary. All this requires complete honesty and integrity. We must tell our friends and supporters what we are trying to do and then try our very best to do it. Some schools may train for competence, intellectually or technically. We must train for competence and conscience, for without the latter we shall surely die of cancer of the spirit.

Great things remain to be done. There is, for example, the separation of the lasting elements in individualism from those factors which were eliminated by the necessities of a complex society. There is a need for a continuing and stronger emphasis on absolute standards of right and wrong as a sure foundation for a living democracy. There must be a revaluation of the place of reason in the life of man. All these are areas in which the Christian college, by reason of its spiritual, intellectual, and cultural background, can do thorough research and make distinctive contributions. Under our American approach to the problems of administration the administrator becomes the key to the solution of many of these problems.

Distinctively and forever we must give our students something true to believe in, something good to live by, and something noble to work for. They must realize even today that they cannot live by bread alone. They are wrong if they still believe that the purpose of education is only to give them a little more bread or a warmer house or a better car. These things are no longer in the saddle to ride mankind to his doom. We now know in a thousand Christian colleges and universities that the only men and women we want on our campuses are those who are willing and eager to embark on the long and lonely quest for something true to believe in, something good to live by, and something noble to work for. It is our task as administrators of Christian colleges at high noon in the twentieth century to affirm that the process of true education can begin and continue only when it is brought into the obedience of the cross. Only in the fellowship of the Eternal can we escape the limiting and cramping of the temporal. He who was Wisdom incarnate and called himself the Way, the Truth, and the Life; who saw all things in the light of eternity; who said, " Every one who is of the truth hears my voice " — he certainly will bless all administrators and teachers and students who humbly seek the truth. He will watch with continuing favor the great quest for truth and beauty and holiness. He will enable us to see again and again, even as the time of man grows late, that we are building the permanent in the midst of the transitory, the eternal in the midst of the earthly, and the holy amid evil. With this vision the administrator of the Christian college can go about his daily work knowing that he is casting bread on far waters and that in space and in time it will always extend far beyond the limits and the weakness of his own life.

# PART
# IV

## *Goals*

# 10

## THE GOALS OF CHRISTIAN EDUCATION

### Kenneth I. Brown

How can we plan intelligently for the national enterprise of education unless there is general agreement among us on the goals for which we plan? By way of introduction, allow me to make three brief comments on our theme " The Goals of Christian Education."

In the first place, the subject of goals is not a once-and-for-all-time subject. It belongs to the " themes of repetition." Periodically, we need to re-examine the objectives we hold for our endeavors, the goals we set for our achievement. College faculties have their annual September gatherings in preparation for the new year — the custom is a wholesome one. Then annually someone in a position of leadership should review the goals of education as they have been agreed upon at his institution and offer critical scrutiny lest they become accepted as tradition, by which, too often, we mean good enough for yesterday but not meaningful for today.

In the second place, the subject of goals is one that must be treated at the various administrative levels. But the complete assignment is not fulfilled until the individual faculty man, faced with his classroom responsibilities in art or sociology or physics, faces squarely and with stout heart the question, What are my goals in this area of education? We must attempt to see the problem in its largeness: the goals of American education, with all its divisions, disagreements, and diversities. But that is only the first level of study. Then must come the review of goals at the next level of classification, when various kinds of institutions may well consider in common their objectives and directions; and next, the institutional study wherein each university, college, and separate department must set forth for its own working blueprint an outline of things to be, for the men in chemistry and the men in economics must particularize, even though there be generalizations to which they might both agree; and finally there is the necessity of the individual instructor's facing for himself the ever recurrent professional question, What are my goals as a teacher? I believe we have need to recognize that the ends of Christian education are different, not in essence but in interpretation, from those of education — education set without a qualifying adjective.

We have need for an adjective to describe those forms of education which we would not include in the generalization of " Christian." The negative " non-Christian," seems to me nondescriptive and quite inadequate. The adjective " secular," so commonly used, has become ambiguous. Dr. Aubrey points out that over twenty-five years the word has been used to refer to nearly everything from scientific humanism, naturalism, and materialism to mass atheism and the depersonalization of man.[1] " Secular " has become too often a wastebasket into which the Christian teacher has thrown his pet peeves. And yet I don't see how we can discard the word until another has been found for the educational situation we are wishing to define. Therefore, in unhappy despair, let me speak of " secular education " as in opposition to what is called " Christian education." Agreeing to use the word, may we stop for a moment longer to remind ourselves that secular education with all its mighty strength — and many of the achievements of education are attributable to secular influences — is concerned more with means than with goals. Secularism can have no goals except as they grow out of popular thought and change with the changes of popular thought, for secularism is essentially the mirror of changing contemporary life. The British educator M.V.C. Jeffreys puts this thought succinctly in the preface to his small volume *Education: Christian or Pagan:*

" The texture of our education is in the main secular. Its aims and presuppositions are secular; it can say nothing of the purpose of human life except that it is what one thinks it is. Consequently, the orthodox descriptions of the alleged themes of education — in terms of citizenship, social adjustment, individuality, self-development, and the like — are really descriptions of means and not, properly speaking, of ends at all." [2]

In the third place, when educators discuss the most important subject of Christian education, there arises the grave danger that, in the enthusiasm for our subject, we shall magnify our differences with secular education and ignore, with serious lack of perspective, our likenesses. That there are differences we shall readily admit. But that there are magnificent and major agreements we must also readily admit. The goals of high scholarship, of competent, well-trained teachers, of well-conceived methods of instruction, are the goals jointly of secular and of Christian education. They are objectives jointly desired and jointly and co-operatively arrived at. In fairness I think it should be said that the present high standards of American education in these regards have come through larger effort on the part of secular educators than by Christian educators, for too often we Christian educators in our concern for our differences have not put the full strength of our shoulder against the wheel of education when education was needing to be freed from the mud of inadequate standards and incompetent scholarship and ineffectual teaching. We need to make it clear that we are not setting up conflicting goals. Rather, as Christian educators, we are insisting that the common goals of education shall be interpreted within larger philosophical and theological perspectives. In essence there is much agreement; and when we differ, it is always with high esteem for the standards of scholarship and for the conditions of great teaching which American education has achieved.

All of us, I am sure, who have struggled to support our educational institutions that have Church connections have suffered from the lack of an accepted understanding among the wide and tolerant constituencies of the Church college of a Christian philosophy of education. It is no denominational pattern we look for. It is not a series of sectarian statements. It is a platform of significant affirmations, growing out of our Christian faith and commitment and applicable to our educational needs.

That interpreter of democracy, Walter Lippmann, has written a merciless book, in which the facts are not prettied up for public inspection. It is an impassioned book, for the author feels deeply about his subject.[3] He is searching for those essential assumptions of human life which shall win the support of rational men. They must include a pattern of fundamental living and thinking which is more than the concoction of finite minds but rather a pattern that is wrought in the cosmos, indigenous to life, and claiming acceptance on the part of thoughtful, reasonable, searching men. He calls it " the public philosophy " and dares to prophesy that unless the Western democracies can rediscover and revive the public philosophy, the days of our democracies are numbered and their fate will be the fate of doom.

If we can dig deep enough to come to some solid rock of understanding as to the nature of educational goals, perhaps we can be of assistance to searching men in Christian philosophy, and we might have suggestions for those who ask how education is represented in the public philosophy.

## The Love of Learning

The first goal of education, both secular and Christian, is the love of learning. A college is composed of groups of people, faculty, students, administration, and its animating impulse is respect for truth, a common search for larger understanding. In the sense that we use the term " learning " we would agree that it is much more than facts and data, no matter how large its measure. I like the definition contained in a recent Princeton publication: " Learning is knowledge which has been shaped by a human understanding and raised by the yeast of creative imagination. It is a state or condition of a human being, rather than an inert possession." [4] I am aware how far this abstract goal of " love of learning " seems from the daily student life of the average American undergraduate. Perhaps one reason for this great divorce is the fact that the learning we so often offer him to love is a kind of two-dimensional sort of thing: facts to be memorized, definitions to be learned, dates to be tacked on the wall of the mind. But lovable learning, although it must include facts and definitions and dates, is more than facts and definitions and dates. Perhaps we have held too much on this two-dimensional level to excite the enthusiasm it rightly deserves. Gordon Allport, the Harvard psychologist, once commented that " with few exceptions, elementary textbooks in psychology distress me by a certain flatness in their treatment of the human mind." [5]

Learning as something to be loved must be three-dimensional; and the third dimension of learning is the element of meaningfulness. It is the honest, critical endeavor to interpret the facts and to re-examine the definitions and to place the dates against the more significant background of the meaning of history. And here is where the Christian educator and the non-Christian will find themselves looking in different directions. For the Christian educator will see the possibility of meaningfulness in learning and the educational experience in terms of the life rather than the career, in terms of ultimate rather than immediate destiny, and in terms of the full man rather than a single corner of mind. For meaningfulness cannot be partial. May I quote again from Mr. Jeffreys, who can say better what I am wanting to suggest.

> " The illumination of the educational process by the Christian sense of divine purpose means, rather, that education is understood and experienced *at its full depth*. The most melancholy feature of our contemporary education, especially our higher education, is its shallowness. It contains a surface layer of knowledge and skill and their relation to occupational need, and social amenity, and it leaves unplumbed the depth of the meaning and purpose in human life. It is cast in the dimensions of preparation for the citizen's journey through some fifty years of wage earning or a professional career, not in the dimensions of the journey of the immortal soul through eternity." [6]

Secular and Christian education may agree upon the goal of the love of learning, but at many points they will be in disagreement in their interpretation of this end. The Christian, holding God as the be-all and the end-all of existence, will see the learning he is invited to love as the partial expression of the mind and the spirit of the creating God; truth, the Christian says, is the nature of God. The secularist will offer his devotion to truth but not within this context. To him the search for truth is a search for truth for truth's own sake. The Christian seeker would add, " And for the sake of the God whom that truth reveals." The Christian will hold his love of learning as an item in his love for God and man; if God be my first devotion, then my commitment to truth, and its expression in human living, will be an integral part of my commitment to God and to love for my fellow man and his welfare. The secularist, founding his life on a differing set of assumptions, will see the love of learning as sources to power and sources to service, but outside any theistic framework.

There is a book published by Harper & Brothers that seems to me to be one of the strong books in this area of Christian education. It is entitled *The Purposes of Higher Education.*[7] Dr. Huston Smith, professor of philosophy at Washington University, is the author. Yet, in a larger way, he is not the author but the spokesman and interpreter for a group of faculty men who over a period of eighteen months struggled with the fundamental questions of the purposes of this intellectual and spiritual experience we call education. The work is in a vein similar to that of *The Crisis in the University,* which bears the authorship of Sir Walter Moberly, but is in part the expression of group searching and group study.

But to return to our thesis: the love of learning must always, according to the Christian educator, be held in a commitment to an utter honesty of search. I do not believe that the secularist has been guilty of less honesty than the Christian; for both, it is hard to see with full vision. For each, there is a predisposition to accept without scrutiny classifications and labels that are half-truths. It is with this fact in mind that I commend Dr. Smith's book. The first two thirds of his study is entitled, " Education Through Six Opposites." Six major dichotomies are listed: absolutism versus relativism, objectivity versus commitment, freedom versus authority, egoism versus altruism, the individual versus the state, and sacred versus secular. The argument runs that as secularists or as religionists we have no right to accept uncritically any of these alternates, with disregard for the truth in the opposite position. By the very hardening of the thought within these "containers," we have made honest search more difficult and the love of learning less attractive.

But it is not enough to speak of a love of learning as if all a man had to do was to shut himself in his library and turn the innumerable pages of innumerable books. Perhaps too often we of the classroom have been guilty of interpreting the love of learning in that kind of indigestive fashion. The love of learning at its fullness demands the championing of ideas, and the willingness to disagree even with the experts, and a giving of oneself to the art of seeking controversy. "The book says . . . but I . . . "; or, "Dr. So-and-So believes this but my experience causes me to wonder." We have good pattern there in the Master's willingness to disagree with the lawgiver of the Hebrew people. It is not the objective of education, whether secular or Christian, to produce "yes men" to the voices of the past, or to dull the edge of adolescent disagreement. And yet, too often our faculty member, consciously or unconsciously, invites the student to give him back his own. I suggest the love of learning as the first goal of education.

### Conserving and Transmitting Our Heritage

There is a second goal that deserves our consideration. Education has the responsibility of conserving the best of our national and international heritage of knowledge, experience, and culture, and of transmitting it to the oncoming generations of learners. Education, if you will, is an initiation into the best that has been thought and said and done and dreamed in the past, but always with the door open to the future and the trust that with knowledge of the achievements of the past more can still be done in thinking and saying and doing and dreaming in the years to come.

There is no novelty in an emphasis upon the importance of the scientific and social and cultural heritage and its transmission as a goal of education. Perhaps the difference between that emphasis as made in 1900 and as made today is in relation to change. Would it be true to state that in 1900 the intent was to conserve the heritage, believing that in it, with minor modifications, were contained the reliable patterns of living? Today the intent is to gather background understanding for decisions adequate for our rapidly changing times, with the thought, not that sacred patterns are contained within the heritage, but that without an appreciative grasp of it we cannot make the judgments and fashion the new courses of action so necessary for our changing today and tomorrow.

But in what way, if any, does the religious-minded educator view this heritage of knowledge and experience differently from his non-religious-minded colleague? Do not both have genuine concern for its conservation, within limits, and its transmission? The answer lies, I think, in the honest insistence of the Christian educator that the past shall be interpreted in its fullness and that that fullness must include the story of religion, its tragic defeats and its glorious victories, its magnificent and its unmagnificent motivations, its role in the drama of man. And the secular educator, with equal honesty, is likely to take one of two positions: either he feels that religion is a museum curiosity, a superstition mothered in primitive man's fear and inadequacy, with possible meaning for yesterday, but little for today and none for tomorrow, or he may espouse the cousin point of view that sees religion as a negativism, religion in its failures and inadequacies, its institutional and human limitations, with nothing worthy of praise. The assumption that religion is wholly negative is sometimes matched by the other extreme, which can be carried to the point of dishonesty by the religionist. The Christian scholar, no matter how great may be the pressures upon him, must not forget that he is a Christian *scholar,* and that scholarship puts demands upon him — demands of gathering all the facts, demands of resolute and impartial appraisal, demands of never withholding unpleasant data or unfavorable judgments. And Christian scholarship, if it be genuinely Christian and genuinely scholarly, will never belittle or negate those demands.

What the Christian educator is asking for is a restudy of our heritage of Western civilization by competent scholars who are not blind to the motivations of religion or heedless of the power of moral and spiritual values to shape human ends. This is no pygmy task. Too often we have talked of " religious perspective " as if it were a quick marriage between the content of the classroom hour and a Sunday school point of view. Nothing can be farther from reality. To teach with legitimate religious perspectives is an achievement more de-manding and more rigorous than to teach with secular perspectives. It requires the scholarly mastery of selected areas of a great heritage and in addition an intellectual and an appreciative grasp of religious truth in a way that makes them an integral unity. I have come to be-lieve that if by religious perspectives we mean something quite apart from our subject matter of teaching, then we are dealing with a hypocrisy that is dangerous to education. However, if by religious perspectives in higher education we are pointing to an integral unity in which subject matter and interpretation are one, then I believe we are thoroughly justified. But achieving this unity will mean hard work: doctoral studies and postdoctoral studies, and the persistent effort of many men to acquire the double mastery of a traditionally secular subject matter and a theology sufficient to give body and strength to religion. Moreover, it must mean the struggle to offer those who are to teach in our public schools a religious literacy which all too often is not theirs today, and for which all too often our teacher-training institutions accept no responsibility. This is not to trespass into that hazardously mined field of " religion in the public schools."

In the spring of 1955 the American Jewish Committee made public in Washington a five-year study on Church-State separation in public schools. They recommended five guiding principles, calling for com-plete impartiality in the realm of religion and the principle of no religious instruction in the school. But one of the five recommenda-tions was this: " Pertinent references to religion, wherever intrinsic to the lesson at hand, should be included in the teaching of history, the social studies, literature, art, and other subjects." As I read this report, it is calling for religious literacy but barring any attempt on the part of the school at religious commitment. It is asking for a presentation of our heritage of knowledge with honest interpretation

of the place of religion in the life of man, neither as wholly affirma-
tive nor as wholly positive, but as that mixture which man has
made it.

A major effort in this field is the five-year study sponsored by the
Association of American Colleges for Teacher Education, Dr. Eu-
gene Dawson co-ordinator, with its fifteen pilot centers where studies
are being made of legitimate ways, with full support of law and
public opinion, for the bringing to the teachers-in-training an awareness of the problem and the opportunity for them to meet it by en-
larging their own religious literacy.

When we speak of the cultural heritage of the past we mean much
more than the records of history, the geological account of the earth's
structure, or science's report of its maintenance and continuing operation. We need the knowledge of yesterday to understand today; and
in ignorance of today how shall we gird ourselves for the conflict
of tomorrow? There have been men in our colleges who shouted,
" Today," so loudly that their voices drowned out the voices of yesterday or the cries of the unborn tomorrow; but they were men of little
vision. They misunderstood education and its gifts for the sons of
men.

If we wear blinders that hold our vision to the immediate hour,
then might we agree with those for whom the mission of the school
is to turn out efficient careerists. (Here I am quoting Lippmann,
p. 78.) Then must we teach the know-how of success and this, sea-
soned with the social amenities and some civic and patriotic ex-
hortation, becomes the subject matter of education. And the student
who applies himself to such a course may conceivably equip himself for success in his career. What more can one ask for? And the
answer comes, Is there no such thing as general knowledge? Where
is the Protestant *Weltanschauung,* by which he shall interpret the
values of his career? Is there no public philosophy for him to possess?
And the troubled Christian educator raises the question, Can his
career be meaningful without the meaningfulness of a religious
understanding of life?

The Communist is scornful; the secularist finds the discussion dreary; the atheist meaningless. And when the Christian presumes to suggest that the tradition of civility, the heritage of our yesterdays, might teach us humility, the Communist and the secularist and the atheist join in their common depreciation of humility. The vice of pride is their most highly proclaimed possession; man is to lose his finitude. And in the new state, according to the Communist, and in his new freedoms, according to the secularist, and in his new divinity, according to the atheist, man can play god. Maybe the Communist state would last were it not for the unredeemed Adam, and maybe the enlarged freedoms of which the secularist boasts might prove salvation for the new man, were it not that the chrysalis of the old man is still entangling him. The old Adam stands ever in need of humility and the humbling knowledge of his finitude. I suggest the conservation and the transmission of our great Judaeo-Christian inheritances as a second goal.

## The Development of the Student

The love of learning is the common impulse of the academic community; the responsibility for sharing the fullest understanding of that-which-has-gone to make that-which-is-with-us more meaningful and to open the door for a better and wiser that-which-is-to-come — such is the responsibility of the academic community. However, a third goal of education deserves recognition, a goal directly and specifically in terms of the individual who is moved by the love of learning and who presumably profits by the increasing grasp of the meaning of that which is past. Education, both secular and Christian, holds for its objective the strengthening of the intelligent individual, the development of a man as a man in his fashioning as a human being. As educators, we are concerned not alone with ideas but with the students in whose minds ideas rest and are reapplied. We are concerned with a meaningful understanding of yesterday, not alone for a right paragraph in a textbook, but for the sake of the man and his society as they must move into tomorrow.

The end product of education is the man. How often we have said that in a thousand different forms! And how often, too, have we spoken and acted on a quite contrary premise: as if the new gym or better campus walks or the new research project were the achievements by which we wanted our institution to be judged! If the end product of education be the man, then the gym becomes important only so far as it may help to develop better men, and the research project only so far as it makes for better men. Administration at the institutional level may well concentrate efforts on two centers: first, the larger recognition that the human product is the sole first goal of education and that all things must be judged thereby; and secondly, the endeavor to bring together the strongest possible faculty — strong in the very ways we hope the student product will be strong — and to keep them strong. That means training and intellectual growth, for faculty and students; for the faculty, sabbatical leaves and further encouragement for study and writing. That means social sensitivity and cultural enrichment for both faculty and students. That means richer, deeper spiritual maturity, not on the level of common agreement, but on that of common search and the common honesty to follow search with faith and commitment.

The student is, indeed, the end product of the colleges; but behind the student stands the faculty member whose influence will be more than the influence of buildings, important though they be; more than the influence of grandiose public relations schemes, although they have their place; more than the influence of football teams and European trips and elaborate campuses, although I am not refusing these things their secondary or tertiary places.

This man, the end product of education, how shall we describe him? We want him to be in the process of fulfilling his intellectual capabilities. But he is more than a brain. We want him growing increasingly in his social sensitiveness and his acceptance of social responsibility. And for him to do so, there must come that development of compassion without which social responsibility is impossible. Norman Cousins writes the stirring words:

" The new education must be less concerned with sophistication than with compassion. . . . It must teach man the most difficult lesson of all: to look at someone anywhere in the world and be able to see the image of himself. The old emphasis upon superficial differences must give way to education for mutuality and for citizenship in the human community." [8]

You may ask for other qualities in this fulfillment of man; I would settle for these three: intellectual progress according to his capacity, social sensitivity and responsibility, and compassion. I offer the student in his growth as the third goal of education.

When one has set forth clearly the goals of education that are to be pursued, the task is not finished until a series of secondary, but nevertheless important, questions have been faithfully answered. Are these goals paper goals for the deception of the public? Or are they the goals that the thoughtful observer would recognize and identify if he saw the day-by-day and the year-by-year effort and planning and partial achievement? Are these the goals of the college president in his ivory tower or even of the sole educator on the board of trustees to whom the trustees look for grandiose enunciation? Or are they goals understood by and acceptable to the faculty, and the alumni, and the students?

There was once a traveler whom they called Educator. And before him lay a journey. For Mr. Educator believed in his heart that in a certain direction was to be found the achievement of his heart's desire. So he prepared himself for the journey, knowing it would be an arduous one. And he mapped his course with care, for the road was devious. But he knew the destination he was seeking. And the friends gathered to bid him farewell. They respected Mr. Educator although they never understood too well all the mysteries he carried in his mind and pondered in his heart. They waved their good-bys. And they turned to one another as he left, saying: " He will get to his heart's desire. He knows the course to take. The goals he is seeking are clear to him. And his direction is toward them."

# II

# THE MARKS OF A CHRISTIAN COLLEGE

## *D. Elton Trueblood*

W E ARE concerned with the philosophy of the Christian college. The great struggle of our time is the struggle of ideas. We have not only outlived the hot war; we have also outlived the cold war. The phrase " cold war " is now obsolete because we are in a third period in which the struggle between the different ways of life is going to be conducted on the strength of convictions. We should, indeed, be happy to participate in the major struggle of our time; however, it is shocking to see how slow the American people are in doing so. In Japan and India the Russians are flooding the country with beautiful books well printed and well illustrated which are often in striking contrast with the pocket books, with their lurid covers, such as we are so familiar with in this country. Sometimes these cheap things are the only output of our minds that the peoples of other countries ever see, in addition to second-rate Hollywood films. Unless we change, we are going to lose out in the ideological struggle.

### OUR REPUTE ABROAD

It is important to know what it is that our critics say about us. Over and over they say three things: first, that we are adolescent; secondly, that we are materialistic; and thirdly, that we are insincere. We are characterized as a people with an immature culture, having low standards in the arts, in literature, and in music. Despite the fact that we pay so much money for it, our education is held in low esteem abroad. Foreign critics often pretend to despise our degrees. Not only the residents beyond the iron curtain but also our friends picture us as materialistic and gadget-minded, concerned only with things and machines, bragging about our ability to make eight million cars in one year. In supporting their third criticism, that we are insincere, they charge that we salute the flag with noble words about liberty and justice for all but do not really mean what we say. It is widely believed that we have two standards of justice, one for the rich and one for the poor, and that we practice racial discrimination. We cannot neglect these criticisms. Effective answers to them are essential, even for our survival, but we cannot answer them merely by words. Obviously we must answer them by our deeds and by demonstrating a kind of life here that carries its own credentials with it.

I believe in the Christian college because I think the Christian college is our most effective agency in the production of a situation in which the three standard criticisms are answered. Our civilization needs centers of creative renewal. These must spring up in the common life of the people who voluntarily establish contrived means of lifting the level of civilization. This is why we emphasize the Christian college. In order to have the power to make the necessary changes in our civilization, we must have a drive as great as a religious commitment; it cannot come in any lesser way. We all know that this is the way most of our colleges began, and it is not likely that we can continue our civilization if it is dissociated from these powerful roots. This is true in regard to our whole conception of civil liberty. Some citizens do not know that our civil liberties have come chiefly from the Biblical view of man, but it is encouraging to find that the President of this great nation understands this very well, and has said so repeatedly.

The question before us is how civilization is to be renewed. We know that many of the criticisms that are leveled against us are just. Some, of course, are unjust, but not all are unjust, and we are wise to have the humility to take them, seriously working at the job of making the requisite changes.

If this philosophy is right, we have in the Christian college something of potential wonder and magnitude. It is important to go on to say that, in many cases, we are failing woefully to live up to the glory of what the Christian college could be. The trouble is not in the catalogues — they all sound so good — but in what goes on in practice contrary to what is printed in them, and it is sometimes both terrible and damaging. For example, there are colleges advertised as having a Christian background in which today the major mood is apologetic about the Christian faith. They try to prove in practice that they are just as worldly as anybody else, with no puritanical nonsense. Often they would really like to ape the State universities, and in some cases they are ashamed of being small. They apparently share the strange notion that bigness and greatness are synonymous. Frequently they lean over backward to prove that they are not pious and that they have become emancipated from religious requirements. They are generous in these matters and demand nothing of their students or their faculty that might not be demanded of any institution of any standing at all. The Christian colleges came about at a great cost, but often we have given them away in wanton waste. This is a shocking thing.

Another great trouble with the Christian college in practice is that it sometimes becomes a scene of bickering and internal jealousy. I recently conversed with a man who had been living close to one of the many Ohio colleges. I asked him how it was getting along. "They're having trouble," he said. "What kind of trouble?" I asked. "Well," he said, "they're having financial trouble. They can't raise enough money. But what is very much worse is that there are fierce antagonisms within the staff." We can say this of more colleges than I wish we could, and sometimes, if the public only knew, the financial problem would be even worse than it is, because people wouldn't knowingly give money to a place where love and unity are not maintained. Sometimes the entire academic community divides sharply between the participants of this crowd and that crowd, with antagonisms that are never overcome. That would be bad enough anywhere, but it is especially terrible where the Christian claims are high.

Another difficulty is that so many of the colleges have low standards. They use religious words, but their students in chemistry really aren't adequately trained to be the equals of other chemistry students when they go out into the competitive struggle. There are Christian colleges in which the important teaching of philosophy is left to some superannuated person not really trained in philosophy. It is the students who are cheated when such things occur; they cannot compete, on a basis of equality, with graduates of better institutions.

The way out is the way of clear vision. We need to know what we are and what we seek to be, and thus, at least, we have a standard by which to judge. We shall not, of course, be perfect in any of these areas, because we are still finite men, and as Christians we know that we are sinners, but there is enormous gain in knowing also what we ought to be and in becoming a factor in the change of events. Let us see, therefore, if we can describe our standard. What are the marks of a Christian college, anywhere?

## Christian Convictions

The first mark is the penetration of the total college life by the central Christian convictions. The important question is not, Do you offer a course in religion? Such a course might be offered by any institution. The relevant question is, Does your religious profession make a difference? Can you show the fruits?

A mere department of religion may be relatively insignificant. The teaching of the Bible is good, but it is only a beginning. What is far more important is the penetration of the central Christian convictions into the teaching of physics and chemistry and English and anthropology and history and sociology and philosophy. The convictions, the interest, and the concern of the professor of psychology may be very much more important for the total life of the college than that of the man who teaches religion, because a man who teaches psychology from a frankly behavioristic point of view is bound to be engaged in the task of undermining what is being said in other areas of a Christian college. The same is true of sociology. There are many sociologists in this country today teaching a relativistic ethics. I do not know whether they are right or wrong, because I am finite, but I do know this: if they are right, the Christian religion is wrong, because the two are incompatible. If a man as an anthropologist teaches the notion that the idea of God is an outmoded, primitivistic conception, even though in his personal life he is apparently a man of devotion, he is the kind of teacher we must reject in making up our staff in the Christian college.

We do not want a theological test; we do not want a church membership test, because that is insufficient. There are people who are church members just by accident or by convenience, but if we apply the test of concern, conviction, and a sense of urgency, we can enjoy the differences in theological emphasis, and we can have a more open-minded group than we can have on any other basis I know. The people who fear Christian dogmatism are old-fashioned and out of date. The worst dogmatism that I have ever experienced is the dogmatism of the unbelievers who do not even imagine that there is any other possible answer than theirs. The Christian by contrast knows that he is in the human predicament. He understands that he is man and not God, and therefore that the greatest possible error is the error of supposing that he is wholly without error. The penetration of total life which we seek will come best by men who have both conviction and intellectual humility, and the gift of passing these on to their students.

### INTEREST IN WHOLENESS

The second mark of the Christian college is wholeness. A college is marked by wholeness when each person in it is encouraged to feel as though he is a part of the entire enterprise. Sometimes in a great university, the people in one department have no concern at all for those in another. If those in another department get into trouble, that's their problem. But the assumption of the Christian college is radically different. In the truly Christian college the physicist will be concerned with helping the historian to succeed. The teaching members will be interested in those who raise the money, and those who raise the money will be interested in those who teach. One of the most damaging developments in our colleges is a worldly division of labor, separating off one group of people called administration and another called faculty, as though they belonged to two different breeds of men. The faculty people go ahead — it's not their problem if the budget is not raised — what do they care? Let the president do it. That's what he was hired for!

No total success can come in this fashion. The only way you can raise the money is for every person to be concerned with the total enterprise. It is not incompatible with the dignity of a professor to raise money. But you cannot do it by standing off in splendid isolation. A division of labor is valid at some points in life, but the Christian faith gives us a grander notion that transcends it, the notion of togetherness. We seek to produce a society that is not a limited liability company, but one in which we recognize unlimited liability for one another. This is a very noble conception and has always been intrinsic in the life of the sacred fellowship called the Church. If the college cannot demonstrate this conception, it is a mistake to call it a Christian college.

### PASSION FOR TRUTH VERSUS DETACHMENT

The third great mark is passion, and here the break with the world is even greater. In the typical worldly institutions the fashionable mood is the mood of objectivity toward every question. There the idea is that a secularist maintains his reputation by standing off in cool detachment. The motto is, " Never get involved; never go out on a limb; don't stick your neck out." Many a professor is unwilling to take a position of his own. He merely reports the positions of others. Above all he keeps cool. But this will not do in a Christian college, because it is essential to the whole Christian idea that there be passion in it. " Though I speak with the tongues of men and of angels, and do not care, I am nothing." The Christian scholar is not merely trying to tell what is the case, though he is trying to tell what is the case; he is also trying to make a kind of life prevail. A Christian is one who is seeking to make the cause of Christ prevail in all of life. Therefore, cool detachment or mere objectivity can never be sufficient for him. Here is where the existentialist conception, so beautifully exhibited in Blaise Pascal's *Pensées,* is really central to all Christian conviction. As Pascal said, " You are embarked." There may not be so much to know, but there is much to be done and much to be loved. You are more than likely to find the truth in many areas by genuine passion than by cool detachment. By the very passion of loving, much is revealed that would otherwise be hidden. This, of course, is the New Testament teaching. Love we are told is the organ of knowledge. " That ye, being rooted and grounded in love, may be able to comprehend " (Eph. 3:17, 18). This is a marvelous conception and it applies to the entire life of the college. If any man is teaching in a Christian college just to have a teaching job, and doesn't feel a passionate conviction, he is certainly in the wrong place and he is mighty foolish to stay.

## The Role of Fellowship

The fourth of these marks is brotherhood. Jesus said, " By this shall all men know that ye are my disciples, if ye have love one to another " (John 13:35). Without this mark a college is not a Christian college at all. It ought to be evident in many ways, including the fellowship not only between students and students, but also between professors and students. Is it the natural thing for the students to go out with the professor over to the coffee shop at the close of the class or lecture? If not, something is seriously wrong. If the professor runs away after class, if he is a " day " professor, there is very little likelihood of the good life appearing. Do the students have a real fellowship with one another? Does this include the foreign students? Does it include students of other races and students of different economic standing? Are the meals really times of growth or are they just times when people eat and run? My guess is that the cafeteria is one of the chief enemies of culture in our day. How wonderful when people can have a dignified meal and sit and eat slowly and be at ease! How good to combine good food with good talk! The great Professor Whitehead has told us that this is how he learned nearly everything when he was a student at the University of Cambridge. He says he had classes in nothing except mathematics, but what broadened him was his experience as he sat at tables with those who were good scholars in other subjects, especially those who were his elders and betters. But now there are colleges where professors eat in separate dining rooms, as if they were afraid that their infection would reach the students. Could anything be more absurd than that? Intrinsic to the idea of the college, and especially the Christian college, is the mingling of life in making up the true fellowship.

It is a shame that we ever got started having what are called fraternities and sororities in the colleges of this country. I do not want to hurt any feelings, but I am really very serious in what I am saying. I realize that sometimes fraternities may have some value, but in the light of my little experience I can affirm that they are evil in practically every way. They are exclusive and snobbish and they break the fellowship where the fellowship needs most to be demonstrated. The fact that they nearly always exclude the foreign students is one of the most deplorable aspects of the situation. What a paradox that we bring foreign students to our country at great expense and then treat them while they are here so that many go back to their homes to become the most bitter haters of America! Their words are listened to because they say, " We lived there four years and never once were invited into a home and they kept me out of their clubs." That kind of criticism is not easy to answer. The total fellowship, then, must be so inclusive that it brings in all kinds and conditions and the affection must be genuine.

### Practical Steps of Achievement

If these are the chief distinguishing marks of a Christian college, our next task is to ask what the practical steps are by which such a pattern may be achieved. This will give us a practical platform.

First we must, as Christians, stress excellence. Holy shoddy is still shoddy. My guess is that we must be more careful about the quality of the work in a Christian college than we are with the work in a State university, because our purposes in a Christian college are so high. You can't pay much attention to a student who claims to be devout and doesn't turn in his papers. You have some reason to doubt the religious experience of a student who murders the English language. It ought to be part of the Christian religion to know the differences between the nominative and objective cases. I realize that it is not in the Apostles' Creed, but it is in mine. It is shameful for people to get college degrees and not be able to get on their feet and say something persuasively. When they cannot, what is the sense in which they are college graduates at all? Some of them may have been clever enough to amass a few credits in the registrar's office, but you've got to be awfully stupid not to achieve that.

The second step is to stress the teacher. Charles Malik, the ambassador from Lebanon, and strong man in the United Nations, at a symposium held at Simpson College used as his text, "Make sure of your teacher and forget about everything else." Now that may be a slight overstatement, but not much. No doubt it is a good thing to have some buildings, but we all know that it is better to have brilliant teaching in shacks than to have sloppy teaching in palaces. The quality of the teacher is more important than the buildings and more important than the curriculum. We say a great deal about curriculum, but the curriculum is not necessarily very important, because the able man dominates it in any case. When a student asked Whitehead what courses he taught, the great teacher replied: " I have three courses. Whitehead *one,* Whitehead *two,* and Whitehead *three.*"

The best story that I know in the history of the American college is that of the way in which the great Timothy Dwight, perhaps the most famous college president whom we have so far had in this nation, chose his first professor of chemistry. Dwight decided, a century and a half ago, that he would add chemistry to the offerings at Yale, so he looked around for an able professor. He met a good many chemists and didn't like any of them, so he did a remarkable thing. He picked out a young man named Silliman, aged only twenty-three, who was brilliant, able, and committed, but had never seen a chemistry experiment. Dwight appointed him professor of chemistry in Yale College and then sent him for three years to London to learn chemistry. Dwight's philosophy was this: A good man can become a chemist, but it is very hard to be a good man. Professor Silliman came back from London and conducted the most brilliant department of chemistry in this nation for fifty years. Today Silliman College at Yale University is named for this man who was first appointed and then trained. This is a wonderful story and if I were the president of a college I would follow Dwight's policy. If I were to find a true fireball, I would hire him even if there weren't any place for him and I had to beg the money to pay him. It is persons of great worth who make a college great.

## ADULT EDUCATION

The third plank in this practical platform is adult education. We must resist adolescence. I recently happened to see the basketball schedule of a good college, in which the president is an eminent educator. It was shocking to find that they played twenty-one basketball games last winter. This seems to me a really sinful thing. Think of all the disturbance. They played two games with nearly every one of their opponents, but *why* I have no idea. Many of the games were scheduled in the middle of the week, disturbing the studies of the other students for no sufficient reason. Here is an artificial encouragement of adolescence. We have perfected these adolescent activities, and then we have put them into the middle of our picture and let them dominate it. The failure is a failure in balance. We ought to keep these pursuits, but keep them where they belong, on the edge of our total life. I know of a college, with underpaid professors, which has had a budget for basketball of $200,000. Is it any wonder that our foreign critics despise our standards?

I should like to put my biggest effort into a course called " Philosophy for Adults," a course in which I could refuse to take any students who were not at least thirty years of age. I wish that all our students were that old. I realize that an eighteen-year-old student could be both intelligent and industrious, but the chances are against it. Usually the very young haven't experienced enough of life to know what it is about. Isn't it a silly thing to limit education to the young? Fortunately, we are now coming to the place where we may change this, because, with modern transportation, there is no reason why people should not go on studying for fifty years. With cars they can gather from a wide area. I predict that the day will come when good colleges will have as many students thirty years old and older as those who are eighteen to twenty-two. I don't see why not. Plato thought that a man really ought to be over thirty before he studied philosophy seriously, and maybe he was right. Of course, we must give the young people a chance, but the point is, we need not limit our efforts to them. The task is so to lift the level that college is not a juvenile pursuit.

The fourth practical undertaking is the production of a religious atmosphere. It is the prevailing atmosphere that determines pretty largely the ultimate conviction of most of the students. This means that you cannot just have one single approach and be satisfied with it. Make your chapel as good as you can, but don't think that that ends the matter. You've got to work through all kinds of groups, through prayer cells, through service activities, through Bible study. In the dormitory make provision for a quiet room. Make the atmosphere of social life and of educational life and of recreational life that in which the Christian conviction is the natural thing, so that it is just like the air you breathe. Then the students will never know the point at which their lives have been deeply changed.

## The Problem of Motivation

The fifth practical task concerns the problem of motivation. The chief reason why education is so difficult for the very young is that millions do not have any adequate incentive for work in college. The liberal arts ideal is a great ideal, which always appears well on paper, but in practice the students often sit and glare at the professor, as much as to say, " Interest me if you can." Because they are being sent, they do not know why they are there. They are not struggling to get somewhere. If we cannot solve this problem, we cannot possibly win. This can be done better by the Christian philosophy than any other way because the Christian philosophy of vocation is one in which we are convinced that our daily work is a holy enterprise. The Christian conviction is that to become a housewife is as much a holy undertaking as to become a pastor, that to enter the ministry of business is as much a sacred calling as to enter the ministry of theology. At least we give lip service to this belief in our great doctrine of the priesthood of the believer. If we were to take this doctrine seriously, it would affect marvelously the whole of our college work. We could give each student a way in which he could combine the liberal and the vocational ideals, for they are not incompatible. The ideal learning situation is one in which a person has a vocational drive that keeps him from being just a drone and at the same time enough judgment to know what he needs in order to be a man as well as an engineer. The perfect situation is that in which the liberal and the vocational purpose are perfectly combined. Nowhere is this better demonstrated than in the vocation of married women.

As President Eisenhower once said, "Now is the time when great things must again be dared in faith." That is a good text for the Christian scholar. You cannot succeed with a little. Try for a little and you won't get even that. Try for greatness, and miracles may occur. The only way in which the Christian college can win in the modern world is by enormously raising its sights. Make no small plans; they have no power to move men's hearts.

# NOTES

Chapter 1

¹ See Jacques Maritain, *True Humanism* (Centenary Press, London, 1938), pp. 37 ff., for a discussion of Communism from the Roman Catholic point of view.

² "Secularism," a statement issued November 14, 1947, by the bishops of the United States. National Catholic Welfare Conference, Washington, D. C.

³ Maritain, *op. cit.,* p. 24.

⁴ *Essays on Catholic Education in the United States,* ed. by R. J. Deferrari. Catholic University of America Press, Washington, D. C., 1942.

⁵ John A. Mackay, *A Preface of Theology.* The Macmillan Company, 1941. Gordon H. Clark, *A Christian View of Men and Things.* Wm. B. Eerdmans Publishing Company, 1952. Émile Cailliet, *The Christian Approach to Culture.* Abingdon Press, 1953. Richard Niebuhr, *Christ and Culture.* Harper & Brothers, 1951.

⁶ W. C. Bower, "Protestantism's Inner Revolt," in *Christendom,* 1937, pp. 290–301.

[7] Reinhold Niebuhr, *The Nature and Destiny of Man.* 2 vols. Charles Scribner's Sons, 1941, 1943.

[8] W. C. Morrison, "Thomism and the Rebirth of Protestant Philosophy," in *Christendom,* 1937. "Theocentric Religion," by H. N. Wieman, in *Contemporary American Theology,* ed. by Vergilius Ferm, Vol. I, pp. 339–351. Round Table Press, 1932. H. N. Wieman and B. E. Meland, *American Philosophies of Religion,* pp. 295–305. Willett, Clark and Co., 1936. "Achieving Personal Stability," by H. N. Wieman, in *Religion and the Present Crisis,* ed. by John Knox, pp. 69–86. University of Chicago Press, 1942.

[9] Richard Kroner, *How Do We Know God?* (Harper & Brothers, 1943) and *The Primacy of Faith* (The Macmillan Company, 1943). Nels F. S. Ferré, *Return to Christianity* (Harper & Brothers, 1943) and *Faith and Culture* (Harper & Brothers, 1946). Erich Frank, *Philosophical Understanding and Religious Truth.* Oxford University Press, n. d. Emil Brunner, *The Philosophy of Religion: Revelation and Reason* (Charles Scribner's Sons, 1937) and *Christianity and Civilization* (Charles Scribner's Sons, 1949).

[10] H. Dooyeweerd, *De Wijsbegeerte der Wetsidee* (The Philosophy of the Law Idea). Amsterdam, 1935. D. H. Th. Vollenhoven, *Het Calvinisme en de Reformatie van de Wijsbegeerte* (Calvinism and the Reformation of Philosophy). Amsterdam, 1933. William Young, *The Development of the Protestant Philosophy in Dutch Calvinistic Thought Since Abraham Kuyper.* 2 vols. Union Theological Seminary Library, 1944. H. Bavinck, *The Philosophy of Revelation.* Longmans, Green & Co., Inc., 1907. "The Possibility of a Calvinistic Philosophy," by H. G. Stoker, in the *Evangelical Quarterly,* Vol. VII, 1935, pp. 17–23.

CHAPTER 5

[1] Gordon W. Allport, *The Nature of Personality,* p. 195. Addison-Wesley Publishing Company, Inc., 1950.

[2] Cf. Ernst Cassirer, *An Essay on Man*, p. 18. Yale University Press, 1944. "But what became more important for the general history of ideas and for the development of philosophical thought was not the empirical facts of evolution but the theoretical interpretation of these facts. This interpretation was not determined by the empirical evidence itself, but rather by certain fundamental principles which had a definite metaphysical character."

[3] The field of psychology seems to present fewer agreements than most sciences today, and the words of Bernard Notcutt in *The Psychology of Personality*, Philosophical Library, Inc., 1954, p. 10, describe a current feeling: "Considering the enormous amount of study and research that have been devoted to the subject, advances in general psychology have been somewhat disappointing."

[4] "The faith in the possibility of science . . . is an unconscious derivative from medieval theology." A. N. Whitehead, *Science and the Modern World*. The Macmillan Company, 1925, p. 19.

[5] V. V. Zenkovsky, "Eastern Orthodoxy," in *The Year Book of Education*, London, 1951, pp. 152, 153.

[6] Arnold Toynbee, *Study of History*, Vol. VII, Oxford University Press, 1954, p. 429, note 2.

[7] It is interesting to note how much modern psychology bases its reading of human behavior on *choices* the interviewed are asked to make.

[8] The writer has tried to sketch the salient points of this misplaced antithesis in an article in *The Lutheran Quarterly*, August, 1954, "Body and Mind in Christian Thought."

[9] *The American Scholar* (Winter, 1952–1953), pp. 50, 51.

[10] Abstract of a doctoral thesis by Lucien White on *Representative French Criticism of Les Rongon-Macquart*, p. 6.

CHAPTER 8

¹ Marie I. Rasey, *This Is Teaching,* p. 5. Harper & Brothers, 1950.

² J. G. Umstattd, *Teaching Procedures Used in Twenty-eight Midwestern and Southwestern Colleges and Universities.* University Co-operative Society, Austin, Texas, 1954.

³ Paul Klapper, " Problems in College Teaching," in *The Preparation of College Teachers,* edited by Theodore C. Blegen and Russell M. Cooper, p. 42. American Council on Education, July, 1950.

⁴ Ralph Harper, "Significance of Existence and Recognition for Education," in *Modern Philosophies and Education, Fifty-fourth Yearbook of the National Society for the Study of Education,* Part I, p. 237. University of Chicago Press, 1955.

⁵ Lauren G. Wispe, "Evaluating Section Teaching Methods in the Introductory Course," in *Journal of Educational Research* (November, 1951) 45:161–186.

⁶ H. S. Maas, "Personal and Group Factors in Leaders' Social Perception," in *Abnormal Social Psychology* (1950) 45:54–63.

⁷ Kenneth E. Clark, and Robert J. Keller, "Student Ratings of College Teaching," ch. 23, in *A University Looks at Its Program,* edited by Ruth E. Eckert and Robert J. Keller, pp. 197–212. University of Minnesota Press, 1954.

⁸ M. M. Trabue, "Characteristics of College Instructors Desired by Liberal Arts College Presidents," in *Association of American Colleges Bulletin* (October, 1950) 36:374–379.

[9] Benjamin Bloom, "The Thought Process of Students in Discussion," ch. 1 in *Accent on Teaching,* edited by Sidney J. French, p. 37. Harper & Brothers, 1954.

[10] Ralph Harper, *op. cit.,* p. 249.

[11] William Hocking, "Dutch Higher Education," in *Harvard Educational Review* (Winter, 1950) 20:31.

[12] Sidney French, editor. Harper & Brothers, 1954.

[13] "Survey of Library Services to Undergraduates," ch. 9 in *A University Looks at Its Program,* edited by Eckert and Keller, p. 103.

[14] Solomon Asch, *Social Psychology,* ch. 16. Prentice-Hall, Inc., 1952.

[15] Stanley Schacter, "Deviation, Rejection, and Communication," in Herbert Festinger *et al., Theory and Experiment in Social Communication,* Part II, p. 51. Institute of Social Relations, University of Michigan Office of Naval Research, 1950.

[16] Richard W. Dettering, "Conformity in Democratic Education," in *Journal of Higher Education,* 26:117–124, p. 124.

[17] Ned A. Flanders, "Personal-Social Anxiety as a Factor in Experimental Learning Situations," *Journal of Educational Research* (October, 1951) 45:100–110.

[18] Lewis Mumford, "The Unified Approach to Knowledge and Life," in *The University and the Future of America,* p. 122.

CHAPTER 10

[1] Edwin Ewart Aubrey, *Secularism a Myth: An Examination of the Current Attack on Secularism,* p. 25. Colgate-Rochester Divinity School, Ayer Lectures, 1953. Harper & Brothers, 1954.

² Montagu Vaughan Castelman Jeffreys, *Education: Christian or Pagan,* p. 7. University of London Press, 1946.

³ Walter Lippmann, *Essays in the Public Philosophy.* Little, Brown & Co., 1955.

⁴ "The Idea of a Princeton Graduate Education," p. 7. Princeton University Press, 1955.

⁵ See Christian Gauss, ed., *Teaching of Religion in American Higher Education,* p. 67. The Ronald Press Company, 1951.

⁶ Jeffreys, *op. cit.,* p. 50.

⁷ Huston Smith, *The Purposes of Higher Education,* Foreword by Arthur H. Compton. Harper & Brothers, 1955.

⁸ Norman Cousins, *Who Speaks for Man?* The Macmillan Company, 1953.

# INDEX

absolutes in standards, 15, 143
absolutism, 152
academic: community, 157, European, 135; disciplines, 37, 25, fragmentation of, 48, 132; freedom, 43, 55, 139, cf. 76, 91, 123
Academy and the Church, 47
administration, 133 ff.
administrators and small classes, 101
adult education, 169
adults, philosophy for, 169
aestheticism, 85
aim(s), 27, 28; as realization of human being, 27; Christ-centered, 130; conversion as, 117, cf. 33, 41; *see also:* ends; goals; objectives
Allport, Gordon, 151, 174
altruism, 152, 153
American Jewish Committee, 155
Anselm, 52
anthropocentric world view, 16
anthropology, Christian, 84
anti-intellectualism, 48
Aquinas, Thomas, 16, 17, 49
Aristotle (Aristotelian), 45, 46
art, modern, 88

asceticism, 87
Asch, Solomon, 129, 177
Association of American Colleges for Teacher Education, 156
assurance of the Spirit and the Word, 61
Athanasius, 82
atheist, 85, 157
" Athens and Jerusalem," 47
athletics, de-emphasis of, 133, cf. 169
atmosphere: classroom, 107, 111, 112, 114, 117, 118, 126; of community, 139; religious, 170
atomism, 19; trend away from, 68
atomistic: irresponsibility, 20; phases of culture, 16
Aubrey, Edwin E., 148, 177
Augustine, 20, 52, 74, 87

Baliol College, 53
Barzun, Jacques, 134
Bavinck, H., 174
behavior of animals as criterion for man, 79
behavioristic point of view, 163
Berdyaev, Nicolas, 47
Bergendoff, Conrad, 79